I0494243

Time

Today's Silent Killer

ROBERTA CAVA

Copyright © 2014 by Roberta Cava

All rights reserved. No part of this work covered by the copyrights hereon may be reproduced or used in any form or by any means - graphic, electronic or mechanical, including photocopying, recording, taping or information storage and retrieval systems - without the prior written permission of the publisher.

Time

Today's Silent Killer

Roberta Cava

Published by Cava Consulting
105 / 3 Township Drive,
Burleigh Heads, 4220, Queensland, Australia
info@dealingwithdifficultpeople.info

Discover other titles by Roberta Cava at
www.dealingwithdifficultpeople.info

National Library of Australia

Cataloguing-in-publication data:

ISBN: 978-1497311817

BOOKS BY ROBERTA CAVA

Dealing with Difficult People
(22 publishers – in 16 languages)

Dealing with Difficult Situations – at Work
and at Home
Dealing with Difficult Spouses and Children
Dealing with Difficult Relatives and In-Laws
Dealing with Domestic Violence and Child
Abuse
Dealing with School Bullying
Dealing with Workplace Bullying
What am I going to do with the rest of my life?
Before tying the knot – Questions couples
Must ask each other Before they marry!
How Women can advance in business
Survival Skills for Supervisors and Managers
Easy Come – Hard to go – The Art of Hiring,
Disciplining and Firing Employees
Human Resources at its best!
Time and Stress – Today's silent killers
Take Command of your Future – Make things
Happen

Human Resources Policies and Procedures
Employee Handbook
Belly laughs for All! - Volumes 1-4
Wisdom of the World! - The happy, sad and
wise things in life!
That Something Special
Retirement Village Bullies
Stressed Out?
Time – Today's Silent Killer

DEDICATION

Dedicated to my support group of loyal friends and family who were always there when I needed them.

ACKNOWLEDGEMENTS

My thanks to Holmes and Richard Rahe for allowing me to use their Holmes-Rahe scale that determines a person's stress level.

Time – Today's Silent Killer

TIME

- Today's Silent Killer

Table of Contents

Brainstorming
Using goal setting plan

INTRODUCTION

Initially, my interest in time management occurred when I found myself financially and emotionally responsible for the welfare of not only myself, but my three children. There just didn't seem to be enough hours in the day to get everything done.

Later, my interest was stimulated when I started my own company. What I did with my time, would decide whether my training and development firm succeeded or failed. But my high energy level caused me to go around in ever-widening circles, starting many projects, but finishing few. I needed to learn how to focus my interest in one direction at a time without being distracted by future tasks and the constant interruptions that plagued my day.

Faced with many conflicting (and often urgent) demands on my time, I developed techniques that gave me maximum benefit from the minimum investment of time. I learned that cutting corners, was not cheating - but rather good management of my time. After I compared how I used my time to how I really wanted to spend my time, I began applying the practical principles of time management. I became energised and was able to accomplish much more than I had in the past.

If you believe time is controlling your life, read this book and start practising prevention.

CHAPTER ONE

Where does the time go?

Time is important in today's society. We make such statements as:

'I don't have time.'
'Time is money.'
'Where did the time go?'
'We save time and waste time.'

We know that referees call time, prisoners serve time, musicians mark time, historians record time and loafers kill time. As consumers, we often invest in labour-saving devices that are really time-saving devices. Union and management discussions often concentrate on: Shorter work week ... flexible hours ... overtime ... double-time ... full time ... part-time ... and permanent part-time.

We sense its importance, but talk about time as if it was something concrete that we could see, feel and hold. If a person from Mars were to hear us talking about time, I'm sure he'd think it was something physical that he could see and

13

touch. In reality, time is our most valuable commodity. If you asked an average eighty-year-old what he cherished most in life, most would state: good health and having more time.

Unfortunately, most of us squander our time. Many spend it existing, rather than living, never realising that life is like a taxi - the meter is always running. When you think of it, the minute you just spent reading this book has gone and will never return. It can't return no matter what you do.

How we use the time we have - whether we waste it just existing or whether we live each minute - depends on each of us. Are you in a rut, just plodding along through life doing things by automatic rote? Then stop your slide into oblivion and ask yourself these questions:

1. Am I doing what I planned to do with my life or did I get off track somewhere along the way?
2. How can I put more 'oomph' into my life so I spend my time living instead of existing?

14

3. Are there things I want to do in my lifetime, but haven't taken the time to plan how I'll make them happen?
4. Do I have concrete, realistic, written-down goals that guide me in the right direction?

Think of life as a journey. If you wanted to take a road trip, you'd likely study the map carefully to determine which route would be the most suitable. You'd spend time planning it. Why is it then, that so few people sit down and plan their lifetime; where they're going and when and how they expect to get there? Instead, many leave it to chance, luck or whatever comes along to determine their life's path.

How are you spending your valuable time? Is it time to make some changes in your life?

How long can we expect to live?

For centuries, society believed that the maximum human lifespan was close to 70 years (the biblical three score and ten). The entire animal kingdom seemed proof that, whether dictated by God or by genes, whether measured in months or years, heartbeats or cell divisions, Earth's creatures seemed destined to live (and die) in highly consistent rhythms: Galapagos turtles within 150 years, elephants within 70, horses in 45, mice in two or three.

All human teenagers enter puberty at roughly the same time; their mothers reach menopause within a similarly small range of years. Such consistency means these basic biological changes must be under genetic control. For all creatures, the ultimate purpose of life is passing on one's genes. After that, there are few evolutionary reasons for sticking around. Pacific salmon for example, die immediately after laying and fertilising their eggs. In humans, similar, though more complex, inborn limits also may make it impossible to boost life expectancy beyond 100. Others believe there are no limits at all, especially if one can enhance the good genes that bestow health and longevity. The encouraging message emerging from new research is that most of what we view as signs of aging - the crippled hands, the laboured steps, the stooped shoulders, are not signs of aging at all, but because of inactivity or disease.

Presently a women's average lifespan is 84 years and rising and men's is 79 years and rising. The gap between men and women's life spans is decreasing because of two major reasons. Women are quitting smoking at a slower rate than men and are sharing the decision-making, which raises their stress level. Because women are sharing the decision-making, men's stress levels are declining.

Unfailingly, studies have shown that when seniors keep active, their lifespan increases. The person who has nothing to get up for is the one who will likely die young.

One radical new conclusion is emerging among some scientists. Rather than aging and dying at a certain point, humans could live to be 200, 300 or more! It may take more than a hundred years to achieve this, but some scientists believe it is possible. With new drugs and genetic tinkering, the odds are good that we could not merely live much longer, but do so in good health. Even if they're only partly right, the implications are staggering. For instance, what would marriage be like, if 'until death us do part' meant 100 years together? Could the workplace employ people for 80 to 100 years? How would our planet overloaded with people now, absorb masses of elders who did not feel a 'duty to die?'

Soon most people can look forward to being alive well into their 80s. Within the next thirty years, half the population in North America will be 65 years of age or older. This should convince you to take care of your body and keep your mind active. By correcting eating or drinking habits, reducing obesity, by exercising and quitting smoking you'll probably enjoy those extra years much more.

We can boost life expectancy with no fancy science at all. Already, with no special tricks, the number of centenarians (people over 100) has doubled since 1980. If we simply reduce deaths from cancer and heart disease, life expectancy could jump. Such a reduction in deaths would impact the baby boomers (our largest population group, born between 1946 and 1964).

The idea there might be no built-in limits to the lifespan is galvanising researchers. For instance, a chemical has reversed brain damage in aging gerbils and extended the lifespan of mice by 20 per cent. This is the equivalent of giving 15 more years to 75 year-old humans. Another drug has rejuvenated the failing immune systems of aged rats so quickly (within 24 hours) that AIDS patients are scrambling for street versions of it. Scientists have rolled back the physiological clock for older men by giving them injections of growth hormone.

Meanwhile, geneticists are searching for genes that could boost human lifespan. A geneticist has found four longevity assurances genes in yeast. When mutated, one gene shortens life; when enhanced, the same gene seems to cause cells to live 30 per cent longer. Pieces of this DNA or genetic material similar to these genes have been found in humans. This suggests that genetic manipulation might lengthen human life as well.

Culturally, it would be a disaster if people lived to age 150 or more. Many who are now in their 80's and 90's wouldn't want to live much longer. However, those attitudes would likely change if the extra decades were years of health and vigour. When baby boomers hit 65 and retire, our already strained health and pension plans could collapse. Some countries have changed the retirement age from 65 to 70, which has made many 64 year-olds very angry.

We worry that increasing life expectancy could add to the time we spend sick and disabled at the end of life suffering from non-fatal, but serious problems (such as severe arthritis, osteoporosis or dementia). Many feel this view is too gloomy; that the same measure that can expand life expectancy will extend the health span as well, compressing disability into an ever-smaller segment at the end of life. The real goal of research is not only to add years to life, but life to years. We wouldn't have a bunch of senior citizens in nursing homes at age 150. We'd probably have people making contributions to society for longer periods, not requiring health care until the late stages.

What is normal aging?

The rate of aging varies enormously among individuals and even among different organs in the same individual. Nevertheless, some changes predictably occur in most humans.

Although it's usually years before we notice, our immune system starts to decline while we're still in our teens. In our 20s, lungs become slightly less efficient and our nerves start sending messages a bit more slowly. By 35, bones stop growing and by the time we're in our 40s, there's no denying it: Time is catching up! Gravity takes hold and as one person put it, 'Everything starts drooping, including my face.'

At this point, kidneys shrink, muscles lose bulk and elasticity and blood vessels begin to narrow. Vision fades and many are forced to buy bifocals. We don't remember things like we used to. We all have physical and mental changes as we grow older:

21

Memory: Treatable:

Most key mental functions diminish only minimally with the years and researchers are working hard to slow or reverse these declines. Physical exercise improves mental function in some older people. Using one's intellect actively throughout life helps others.

Overall, the brain's ability to process information does slow as we age. However, when we give most healthy elderly people enough time and an environment that keeps anxiety at bay, they can score about as well as young or middle-aged adults on mental tests. The elderly may not learn or remember quite as rapidly, but they may learn and remember nearly as well. In most people, the capacity to focus on a task or follow an argument is also well-maintained throughout life. The chief decline in healthy older people is their ability to perform several tasks at the same time or switch back and forth rapidly between tasks. They can overcome this, by organising their work so they can focus on one task at a time.

Memory: Untreatable

For many people, the most dreaded aspect of aging is not the chance that the body may falter, but that the mind (the core of one's personality) may shrivel into nothingness. There are, sadly, many ways to lose one's mind. A few of these are; strokes, Parkinson's disease and severe depression. However, the sinister ailment that realistically terrifies many is the progressive, irreversible dementia called Alzheimer's disease. By age 85, a study showed that 47 per cent of people have enough symptoms to meet the definition of Alzheimer's. Other researchers, using different criteria, put the figure closer to 20 per cent.

People suffering from Alzheimer's disease have difficulty in communicating with others. Some cannot make themselves understood or don't understand others. They may become angry or defensive if they can't find the words to answer questions. They forget information within seconds. Some can read words, but fail to understand those words. Others may understand face-to-face encounters, but fail to understand phone conversations.

Eventually, they lose their sense of direction and become lost. The route they took to the corner store is suddenly unfamiliar to them. They forget where their bedroom is in their homes. Others try to put cakes into the dishwasher to bake, put milk in the cupboard and sugar in the fridge. (We've all shown these signs from time to time, but only in isolated incidents.) Alzheimer's patients often live in the past. Some believe their sons (who may resemble their fathers) are their long-departed husbands and talk to them as if they were. Unfortunately many caregivers forget that the patient may understand more than they think and talk about them as if they weren't there.

There is encouraging news for those with severe cognitive losses. Scientists are finding that experimental new drugs (especially a compound called nerve growth factor) can trigger brain regeneration.

Personality: A person's personality does not have any radical changes after age 30 unless the person receives psychotherapy. This is particularly true in individuals who've lived in abused relationships, either during childhood or as young adults. Many continue to live in the past, locked into passive personalities or become aggressive themselves as a response to the violence they believe is normal in everyday interactions between people. Personality changes also occur if the person develops a dementing illness.

Sense of smell: This starts to decline slowly at age 45, but escalates at a faster rate after the person reaches 65.

Thymus: When a child enters puberty, her thymus begins shrinking and his/her immune response begins a slow decline.

Lungs: There is a 40% drop in maximum breathing capacity between ages 20 and 70.

Muscles: With lack of exercise, 20% to 40% of muscle mass is lost between age 20 and 90. Exercise prevents most of this loss.

Ovaries: After menopause, a woman's body dramatically slows production of estrogen.

Blood vessels: The diameter of vessels narrows and arterial walls stiffen and there is a 20 - 25% increase in systolic blood pressure.

Pituitary gland and hypothalamus: Secretion of growth hormone declines at age 50, causing muscles to shrink and fat to increase.

Sight: The ability to see nearby objects declines at age 40, but the ability to see fine detail does not deteriorate until age 70.

Hearing: This begins to decline around age 20, but decreases faster in men than women.

Bones: After the age of 40, bones begin to weaken and many suffer from osteoporosis. The decline is more prevalent in women.

Heart: There's little decline in resting output, but a 20% decline in maximum rate during exercise occurs after a person reaches 40. At this stage the heart becomes less responsive to stimulation from the nervous system.

Adrenal Glands: After age 30, secretion of DHEA (which slows cancer and boosts immunity) declines and after 70, production of the stress hormone cortisol soars.

Skin: There are changes in collagen (a connective tissue) which causes the person's skin to lose elasticity in later years.

Nerves: Between age 40 and 80, the speed of messages along nerves drops 10%.

Having a strong will is one key to living longer. People who live to healthy old ages have several characteristics in common: a good immune system, a balanced lifestyle and a strong personality. Learning how to manage stress is important for a long healthy life. Bad stress leaves a person feeling angry and hostile. Chronic stress can compromise the immune system and lead to anxiety disorders or depression, all of which can reduce longevity.

Immune system: Whether you have a good immune system or not is mostly the luck of the draw. If your parents weren't susceptible to infections, if they were sufficiently healthy most of their lives, chances are good you'll enjoy the same robust health.

In the same way, we can inherit many diseases related to a defect in the immune system, such as certain types of diabetes. The immune system also changes as we age. Cells in people aged 75 and older take longer to produce the antibodies that fight infection. It takes about seven days for the cells in a young or middle-aged adult to produce the antibodies that fight infection. It takes the cells in elderly people between 14 and 21 days. This probably accounts for elderly people being more likely to suffer infections that require hospitalisation.

Strong personality: Several personality traits contribute to a strong will, but two important ones are self-esteem and a sense of purpose. Such people believe in their ability to make things happen for themselves. Obstacles don't stop them and they're more likely to keep going at it. But those with low self-esteem blame themselves when things go wrong and stop trying. Reminding themselves about what they could have done or should have done better gets them nowhere.

Some psychologists say self-esteem goes back to the kind of bond you formed with your parents as a child. Maybe it does, but studies show that you can improve how you feel about yourself. But that's another book.

How to live a longer, fuller life

Aging is far more under our control than we once thought. Chronological age is now considered a bad marker of biological age. Heredity may account for up to 30% of change to vision, hearing and reaction times. You can't do much about that. However longevity is due to one's lifestyle, chiefly exercise and diet.

Although that message is important for people already in their later years, it's particularly crucial for people in their midlife years (the baby boomers). The changes that are observed in the aged are clearly long-term processes that start in midlife. The baby boomers are the first generation to enter midlife with information they can use to guide their behaviour and control their own aging.

In addition to exercise and diet, statistically there are several tricks to longevity. The first is to choose good parents with a good set of genes. Skip those with genes that result in fatal childhood diseases or predispose you to cancer or heart disease. Instead, choose rich, well-educated parents, which will lessen your chance of dying in infancy.

After you pass your toddler stage, the trick is to dodge bullets, cars, high stress and AIDS for the next 44 years. Up to age 45, accidents, homicides and suicides are the biggest killers. AIDS is gaining. Car fatalities often involve alcohol or passengers who did not wear seat belts. So if you drink, don't drive - and wear your seat belt. If you ride a bicycle or motorcycle, wear a helmet.

Violence is still a big killer as you move from your 20s into your 30s. If you feel hopeless or depressed, get help. A fatal combination for himself and others is to allow a desperate person to have access to a gun. Angry people are three and a half times more likely to have a heart attack; four times more likely to get cancer.

If you've reached the ripe old age of 45, congratulate yourself on making it through the first big statistical minefield. There are many other dangers facing you now. If you're a smoker or overweight, change your ways. The future yawning before you is stocked with big chronic illnesses, chiefly cancer and heart disease. It's here that lifestyle begins to kill you or save you.

You've reached 65 - congratulations again. Once you make it this far, the odds for a long life get better and better. If you're a woman, the odds now are you'll make it to age 84. At birth, the odds were only 79. If you're a man, the odds now are that you'll likely reach 79. At birth your life expectancy was 72. Keep exercising or start exercising and eat a sensible diet. If you don't - keep praying. By age 85, you're a statistical marvel. The odds of making it to 91 are now 50-50. How far you've come! At birth, the chance of reaching 101.5 was only 1.5 per cent!

Why do we age?

People accept aging like they accept their car wearing out, but living organisms can repair themselves. So why do we age?

In the wild, aging is rare because predators often make long life impossible for many. However, for humans, who have learned to beat back predators (including viruses and bacteria) the question of why we age at all is keeping researchers busy.

One theory states that living to an old age results from human's delayed reproduction cycle. Animals that mature slowly and wait years to reproduce often live the longest after reproduction. Genes that foster late reproduction, automatically eliminate genes with early detrimental effects. Estrogen, for instance, is essential for reproduction in females. Unfortunately, after reproductive years end, estrogen can trigger breast cancer. Similarly, testosterone helps males build muscle for winning and defending turf, but can be the cause of late-life prostate cancer.

There's proof that being able to laugh at life helps increase longevity. Those who are jovial and happy live longer, more productive lives. The following might give you your chuckle for the day:

You know you're growing old when ...

- Everything hurts and what doesn't hurt doesn't work.
- The gleam in your eye is from the sun hitting your bifocals.
- You feel like the night before and you haven't been anywhere.
- Your little black book contains only names ending with M.D.
- You get winded playing cards.
- Your children begin to look middle-aged.
- You finally reach the top of the ladder and find it leaning against the wrong wall.
- You join a health club and don't go.
- You begin to outlive enthusiasm.
- You decide to procrastinate, but never get around to it.
- Your mind makes contracts your body can't meet.
- A dripping faucet causes uncontrollable bladder urge.
- You know all the answers, but nobody asks you the questions.
- You look forward to a dull evening.

- You need glasses to find your glasses.
- You walk with your head held high, trying to get used to your bifocals.
- You turn out the lights for economic, rather than romantic reasons.
- You sit in a rocking chair and can't get it going.
- Your knees buckle, but your belt won't.
- You regret all those temptations you resisted.
- You stop looking forward to your next birthday.
- After painting the town red, you have to take a long rest before applying a second coat.
- People start calling you a Senior Citizen.
- You remember today, that yesterday was your wedding anniversary.
- You can't stand people who are intolerant.
- The best part of your day is over when the alarm clock goes off.
- You burn the midnight oil after 9:00 pm.
- Your back goes out more than you do.
- A fortune teller offers to read your face.

- Your pacemaker makes the garage door go up when you watch a pretty girl walk by.
- The little old grey-haired man you help across the street is your husband.
- You have too much room in the house and not enough in the medicine chest.
- You sink your teeth in a steak and they stay there.
- You wonder why more people don't use this print size.

Does having money make a difference?

Despite a generation of Medicare, the gap in life expectancy between the richest and poorest has narrowed only slightly. It may not buy happiness, but money adds four more years to the lives of the 20 per cent of people who live in the richer neighbourhoods.

The poor face barriers even before they're born. Babies born into poor families are more likely to be premature, smaller and have lower birth weight than richer babies. Many are born to teenage mothers without the income, diet or support they need. Though today's babies are getting much better care than they did a generation ago, the gap between the rich and the poor persists. Wealth provides proper nutrition, secure social support, comfortable housing in neighbourhoods more free of pollution and violent crime, safer motor vehicles and other safety devices.

Richer people are more likely to have families, friends and supporters that are important to health. They're more likely to get a good education. They have challenging jobs free of accidents and toxic fumes and the time and resources to fight everyday stress. Their jobs offer more security and opportunities to develop skills, exercise control or manage their time.

Somehow, a lesser start in life seems to lead one to make poor decision-makers when it comes to smoking. Sixteen per cent of the poor are heavy smokers compared to eleven per cent of the general population. Interestingly, the poor were less likely, to drink alcohol than the rich and they are less likely to drink and drive. When they do drink, they're more likely to do so to overcome stress or depression. They're also twice as likely to use tranquilisers and sleeping pills as the rich. The poor are less likely to use seat belts or wear motorcycle or bicycle helmets. Low-income women are less likely to have Pap smears and perform breast self-examinations.

Retirement

To many people, the word 'retirement' makes them rub their hands with glee. Others become depressed, because to them, it means the end of their productive lives. Those in their middle-aged years (40 - 55) should be seriously thinking of what they'll do with their lives when they retire.

Statistics now prove that men can retire earlier and with fewer cares than women. Only 70 per cent of men and 51 per cent of women have a pension plan. Women traditionally enter the work force later than men and have built up less in their pension funds. Working women don't plan to retire or retire as early as men do, unless they marry and their husbands have a good income.

An emerging trend shows that when husbands retire, many of their wives decide to stay in the workforce. The women's reasons for doing so relate to money (or lack of it) medical and pension benefits, job satisfaction and a sense of identity. Their husbands may have been in the workforce for 45 years but many wives (five to fifteen years younger than their spouses) have worked for 25 or 30 years. They aren't ready to retire.

Women who marry older men or marry for a second time may still be in the middle of their career paths when their husbands retire. Many husbands object to the reversal of traditional roles where they're the homemaker and their wives are the breadwinners. Power struggles often occur, which can affect the man's ego. Couples who are approaching this milestone in their lives should look carefully at the upheaval this might cause in their relationship. They should take steps to lessen the perceived problems - *before* retirement.

Divorced women spend three more years in the work force than married or widowed women.

This shows that women usually come out of a divorce worse off economically than a man. Widows can collect from their husband's pension fund as well as from their own. Unfortunately pension funds are not as kind to divorced women. They end up with only one pension fund to count on. Many are exempt from receiving benefits from their ex-spouse's pension fund. Canada corrected this inequity by providing for a fair division of pensions for women obtaining a divorce after the year 1977. Women who divorced before that date are not allowed this benefit.

How much time do we have?

Have you ever considered how much time you have to do all the things you'd like to do in your lifetime? In the following information, I've shown total hours and days for a lifespan of 75 years. At the beginning of the twentieth century, the average man's life expectancy was 46. This meant that if you were 23 years of age, you were middle-aged! Here are some facts that might interest you.

There are:

- 24 hours in a day
- 1440 minutes in a day
- 168 hours in a week
- 8,760 hours in a year
- 657,000 hours in 75 years
- 27,375 days in 75 years

Time breakdown

What does the average person do with his or her personal 168 hours in a week? One North American survey identified that the average person spent his or her time as follows:

Activity and hours:

- Sleep: 56
- Personal Hygiene: 7
- Eating: 7
- Travel: 5.25
- Work: 66.5
- Pleasure: 9
- Self Improvement: 1.75
- Illness: 1.5

TOTAL: 150
Hours left: 18

The above survey shows that the average person sleeps eight hours a night. How many hours do you sleep per night? Is this through choice or necessity? Do you feel you need more sleep to feel fully rested? Less?

If you said you needed more sleep, could it be because life is so boring that you regularly choose sleeping as a way of spending your time? If this is the case, get more challenge into your life. If you wake up before your alarm goes off in the morning, it's probably because you've had enough sleep. (Get more information on this topic in Chapter 10 on Sleep and Fatigue).

Personal Hygiene includes bathing, shaving, putting on makeup or combing your hair. Eating, counts only the hours you spend actually eating, not those spent preparing the meal, cleaning up after it or socialising during the meal.

Travel is all the travel you do during the week including driving to work, doing grocery shopping, running errands and driving yourself or your children to activities.

Work, includes paid and unpaid work. Women's total in this area is normally much higher than men's.

Pleasure, includes watching television, reading a book, participating or watching sports or going to a party. This is the area of your life where you let your 'little kid' out to have some fun. An important part of your life is having fun: don't neglect it. Plan these activities, so you don't cheat yourself in this area.

Self-improvement includes all the time you spent at regular school as well as any courses you've attended since then. This includes reading non-fiction books, receiving in-house training at your place of employment and other developmental activities.

Illness (self explanatory)

We've accounted for 150 hours of our week. What are we doing with the 18 hours we can't account for? We spend it waiting for something or someone or just goofing-off (which may be necessary under some conditions).

How do you spend your time? To determine what you really spend your time on, complete the following information for one week. You may find some surprises. Possibly you're spending more time watching TV than you thought you did. You might decide to spend that time more constructively towards reaching your goals.

Minutes per week and percentage:

1. Sleep
2. Personal Hygiene (washing, hair, makeup, shaving)
3. Eating
4. Travel (commuting)
5. Work (salaried) (home, shopping, cooking, cleaning)
6. Pleasure (TV, sports, reading)
7. Self Development (education study)
8. Illness

Decide the %age of time you spend at or with:

a) Working
b) Family
c) Social (community)

d) Goof-off time or illness

I often have couples that attend my time management sessions together and I encourage them to complete the above questionnaire. After they completed the questionnaire, one couple decided to make some drastic changes in their lives. They lived in an older home with eight rooms (they'd had a large family) on an acreage out of town. Both of them worked weekends in the summer growing a market garden. Most of their spare time disappeared in just maintaining their big house and land.

Each spent almost three hours a day getting to and from work. (On an average working day, most people spend ten hours a day, getting ready for, travelling to and working at a job). Their last daughter was just leaving home to attend university, so there was no further need for them to keep their large house.

What the couple really wanted to do was travel. But they couldn't leave their property unattended for long periods. They sold their rural property and moved into a high-rise condominium in the city. This meant that they spent only fifteen minutes travelling to work and were free to lock their door and travel when they wished. No longer did they have to cut grass, tend their market garden or shovel snow. An additional plus was that they had a smaller dwelling to care for, so could enjoy their time off after their work days.

Another man felt discouraged because he wanted to advance his career by taking courses in the evenings. He felt he didn't have time because of his busy lifestyle. After completing the questionnaire, he found that he spent 24 hours a week watching television! He decided he did have time to take the courses he required.

Fear of failure

People's attitude to life keeps many from making full use of the years they have. Many turn down excellent opportunities but can't explain why they've done so. If this happens to you, ask yourself, *'Why am I not taking this opportunity?'* Is fear of failure holding you back? Or is it lack of money, connections, time or possible family problems? Learn to analyse why you're being your own worst enemy.

Offer some people promotions and they automatically assume they're incapable of handling them. They'll think of every situation where they can't possibly measure up. They'll often turn down a promotion because of their fears. Unfortunately, if they *do* accept the positions and still have these negative feelings, they're probably setting themselves up to fail.

I know people who have sat on the fence wailing about their problems for so long, they're afraid to get off and begin living. I call them Mugwumps. Mugwumps are those who have their mugs on one side of the fence and their wumps on the other. They've got to get off that fence! All you get from fence sitting; is slivers.

These people don't comprehend that they're putting themselves under more and more stress the longer they're on that fence. Not deciding becomes more stressful than deciding. Think back a bit. When you had a tough decision to make, wasn't it stressful? Do you remember the relief you felt when you finally took the step and made a decision? The tension goes somehow. Fence sitting is very draining as people mentally bounce from one solution to another, without deciding which decision is right.

Anyone can overcome the fear of failure by keeping in mind that they're capable of accomplishing far more than they believe they can. In a work situation, I recommend that no one should take a promotion if they know every aspect of the job. If they do this, they're already overqualified for the position. All promotional opportunities should leave room for the person to grow and learn while on the job or through additional training.

We need courage to take risks, but life without risk is very mundane and boring. Some fear not being able to pull it off - that they'll fail. They believe that failure is bad, so in taking risks, they're facing the chance of ending up with not one, but two bad feelings. These are their failure at what they tried to do, plus their lowered self-esteem. If you wait until 'you're in the mood,' you may wait an eternity before reaching your goals.

I always approach new challenges with an open mind. When approaching a new task, I rationalise, 'I've never tried this before - but I'll try my best.' I resist feelings of panic if I don't do something well (and know I've given my best try). Instead, I acknowledge that this is something I don't do very well. Then I try something else. If I *do* succeed at the task, the positive results usually spur me on to try other new challenges. The momentum of my success keeps me 'up.' With this positive approach, I find that three out of five things I try, I succeed at and the ratio is improving.

Fear of success

Everyone has their personal definition of what success means to them. I feel successful when I set goals and achieve them. What would it take to make you feel successful?

Do you feel that if you become a success you might lose the love and comfort of important people in your life? Do you feel you might outgrow your close friends? Do you feel that your success might force you to find new support groups and friends? If you choose to start climbing, you may feel an obligation to keep climbing. You may not be sure how high you can climb. You'd hate to fail along the way. Some feel this would be worse than not trying in the first place.

Men are far more comfortable with success than women, because they're expected to succeed. Some women have the definite fear that they **will** succeed. This is often a well-hidden fear and their actions to thwart their success are also well hidden. Successful females often appear more competitive than the average woman. You may feel uncomfortable in this role. Will people think you're less feminine if you succeed? Many men feel intimidated by successful women and give put-downs you might not be able to handle.

Married women may be afraid that they might make their spouse feel uncomfortable with their success. Or their fear may be that they'll lose their mate. Single woman may feel that the number of available men willing to accept a successful female is too low for their liking.

Other women may feel they may have to choose between being successful in a career and having a spouse or mate. Some feel that they can have one or the other, but can't have both. (The majority of women have both).

When I started climbing the corporate ladder, I made a conscious decision to stop holding myself back. No longer was I afraid of stepping on others' toes with my competency and no longer did I feel the necessity of acting like a 'dumb blond.' This was very threatening territory, but it wasn't worth the pain of holding myself back. I had spent years back-pedalling and trying not to offend people who were more senior than myself.

Self-sabotage

People often blame others when they don't get what they want. But the reason they fail is not as obvious - they sabotage their own efforts. There's a 'little twerp' inside us who asks maliciously 'Who do you think you are?' and questions our every action. When these ideas take over, they block the good feelings we have after a job well done. Instead, we concentrate on some little task we've done wrong.

Do you let yourself feel that you've failed at something, when you've given it your best attempt? Early in life, I learned to take the word 'failure' out of my vocabulary. Tell yourself that you just didn't succeed at it. Make it a learning experience, rather than expecting yourself to be perfect. You can't be good at everything! If you think you have to be, you're likely going to spend most of your life in misery.

If you're holding off doing something because you're afraid to take the risk, do the following:

a. Define as closely as possible, what you think the risk is.
b. Determine what you could gain emotionally and physically by trying it.
c. Determine what you could lose emotionally and physically by trying it.
d. Do you need more information before taking the risk? Where would you get this

information? Who has this kind of information?

e. How could you lessen the risk?

f. Is it now worth taking the risk?

A more simplistic method is to ask yourself two questions before trying something that's possibly risky. These questions are:

What have I got to gain?

What have I got to lose?

If you have much to gain and little to lose, it's foolish not to try. To get yourself started, identify some of the things you do well. Do you excel at swimming? Try snorkelling or SCUBA diving. Any time you try something that is close to the activities at which you excel, your likelihood of success is increased. If you're a musician, try another similar instrument. This will boost your self-esteem level.

CHAPTER TWO

Time management techniques

The Busy Man: Author Unknown

If you want to get a favour done by some
obliging friend,
And want a promise safe and sure on which
you may depend,
Don't go to him, who always had much leisure
time to plan,
But if you want your favour done, just ask the
busy man.

The man of leisure never has a moment he can
spare;
He's busy 'putting off' until his friends are in
despair;
But he whose every waking hour is crowded
full of work,
Forgets the art of wasting time - he cannot stop
to shirk.

So when you want a favour done and want it
right away,

53

Go to the man who constantly works 20 hours
a day.
He'll find a moment somewhere, that has no
other use,
And fix you while the idle man is framing an
excuse.

Principles of time management

Time management works no matter what kind
of situation you're in. Whether you work in an
office, a warehouse, in the home or out in the
field, use these in your management of time.

1. Plan effectively. Every hour spent in
   effective planning saves three to four in
   execution and achieves better results.
2. By failing to plan, you're planning to fail.
3. Plan early. Daily planning, formulated
   either the afternoon before or early the
   same day, is essential to effective use of
   personal time. (Do you spend some time
   planning your day?)
4. Budget or assign time to tasks in direct
   relationship to their priority.
5. Impose deadlines on tasks or decisions and
   exercise self-discipline in following them.

This helps overcome indecision and procrastination.

6. Group similar tasks within divisions of the work day. (i.e.: making all your phone calls at one time).

7. Keep a daytimer or To Do list and use it faithfully.

8. Remember Murphy's Second Law, 'Everything takes longer than you think,' especially if you delegate the task, so make allowances for this.

9. Consider waiting as a 'gift of time' - use it, don't waste it. Be flexible in scheduling your time to consider forces beyond your control.

10. Avoid surprises by expecting the unexpected and plan for it. Assume that if anything can go wrong, it will. (Murphy's Third Law). Anticipatory action is usually more effective than remedial action. A stitch in time saves nine.

11. Don't over-estimate problems and treat all problems as if they are crises. Upon investigating crises you'll probably find they're mostly low priority items.

12. During the day, ask yourself *'What's the best use of my time, right now?'*

Are you over-planning your day?

Do you find that your problem is that you plan your day down to the last minute without considering that you might spend 30 - 40 per cent of your time just 'fighting fires' and helping others. Do you find there are always tasks still to do at the end of the day? Is your day nothing but interruptions and crisis? Don't schedule every minute of the day with appointments; save some uncommitted time.

Keeping a time log

This will identify your constant interrupters. In business this could be a simple entry such as: Bill Jones - talked about Miller Account, 5 minutes. Mary Smith - needed figures for the budget, 10 minutes. Apply the 80/20 rule. 80% of the calls will be coming from 20% of the callers. Consider setting a special time for calls or to have a personal assistant screen them. Or assign calls to someone else. If you repeatedly spend a lot of time on the phone with the same people, try to find a time to handle all the person's problems at once.

At home, do friends often telephone or drop in unexpectedly? If it's a telephone problem, keep the caller informed about your time constraints. If they drop in, ask them to call first.

How to choose priorities

Whether you plan your day the afternoon before or early in the morning, choose what is most important. Rank items from A to D. Do the A's (which are usually more difficult) first. Getting them done will increase your self-esteem. Don't let an easy C task get you off track.

- **Priority As** - Important and urgent, must be done right away.
- **Priority Bs** - Important but *not* urgent, can be done now or later.
- **Priority Cs** - Often urgent to others, but of low importance to you.
- **Priority Ds** - Garbage, throw away.

Now consider how you plan your time. Do you use:

1. Daytimers and 'To Do' lists, or
2. To keep track of appointments do you use:
   (a) A desk calendar?
   (b)   A daytimer?
   (c) Use another (possibly more complex) system?
3. How effective do you find your personal system?
4. Do you make 'To Do' lists every day - even on weekends?

It's important that you consistently use whatever system works best for you. And I stress the word 'consistently.' Try a variety of methods to show which one works best for you and stick with it. My philosophy is, *'If it ain't broke - don't fix it,'* so if you're happy with your present system, keep it up.

I use both a daytimer and a 'To Do' list. When a company hires me to do a seminar, I write down everything I have to do for their seminar on a separate 'To Do' list. I then put dates next to the tasks and then put the information in my daytimer. Using this method, I seldom forget anything and have a back-up list that I can tick off when I complete the activities. For example, my daytimer would have entries on when I would send a training contract and when a signed copy should be returned; book airline tickets when contract was confirmed, etc.

You can imagine what would happen if I forgot anything such as:

Forgetting to tell a company that I required a PowerPoint projector so I could show my slides or forgetting to make travel arrangements until the last minute. For me the dual 'To Do' system works well. What alternate system might work for you? Once you decide, use it faithfully.

Different kinds of tasks:

Try to see which of these tasks cause you the most difficulty (possibly because there are so many of them):

1. Simple short-term tasks:
   These are routine activities found in any job. These tasks are simple and short-term in nature, which can occur frequently.

2. Complex short-term tasks:
   These are complex, but require only short-time effort for accomplishment. They require an intermediate level of planning and effort.
3. Simple long-term tasks:
   These are simple, but require long-term effort to complete. These tasks also may need an intermediate level of planning, due to the long-term effort required to complete them.
4. Complex long-term tasks:
   These take a high level of effort and planning and are often avoided in favour of a less complex task.

Did you identify either #1 or #3 as those that gave you the most problems? If you're a supervisor and these tasks are so simple - why aren't you delegating them downward? Could you pass some of those tasks on to your staff or family members? On the job, this would allow you to do the more important tasks you're paid to accomplish.

Swiss cheese approach

Large blocks of uninterrupted time are a comparative rarity. If again and again (a few minutes before lunch, etc.) you choose to work on an unimportant task rather than begin a difficult, important task, then you're procrastinating. You're avoiding what's really important.

One way to tackle complex long-term tasks is to use the 'Swiss cheese' approach (this is the cheese with holes in it). Take 'little bites' out of your long-term task (instant tasks).

Instant tasks can take from one minute to an hour to accomplish. Most are ten minutes or less. What might appear at first to be instant tasks, often turn out to be groups of tasks that you could divide into smaller 'bites.' After each instant task, you would identify the time it would take to complete it.

In your planning you might have several group tasks that can be broken down into instant tasks. For example: Your task is to hire three new employees. Two sample instant tasks could be:

1. Obtain the job description of the position - 2 minutes
2. Write an advertisement for the newspaper - 15 minutes

The following are group tasks that have been broken down into instant tasks:

1. Screen one resume or application form - 5 minutes (a group task would be reviewing all of them)
2. Set up one appointment - 5 minutes
3. Conduct one interview - 45 minutes
4. Evaluate one candidate - 7 minutes

Using this method, you could fit small instant tasks throughout your day as time permits. For instance, if you were waiting for a phone call or had to go to a meeting in five minutes, you could screen one resume or application form.

Try the Swiss cheese approach in family chores as well. For instance removing wallpaper from the wall and painting the room takes planning. You don't have to do this task all at once. Instead, do it in bits and pieces (instant tasks). Removing the furniture from the room is a group task. Removing one piece of furniture from the room could be an instant task. Covering the remaining (immobile) furniture with drop sheets is another. Sloshing hot water on the existing wallpaper is another. After wetting down the walls a few times (group task) it's time to strip off one strip of wallpaper (instant task). This is how you can fit tasks in at home as well.

How to start complex long-term tasks:

Suppose you're responsible for setting up your company's annual meeting (not their annual report) and can expect about 150 people to attend.

1. Choose several 'Instant Tasks.'
2. Set a time estimated to complete each task.
3. Determine obstacles you could run into while completing each task.

Here are some suggested instant tasks.

1. A group of tasks is to check all hotels for availability. An instant task is to contact

one hotel to see if they have facilities available when you want them. Also ask what accommodations they have available for any out-of-town guests. The next instant task would be to call another hotel.

Time: 15-20 minutes

Obstacles: Person was not there, could not get information on first call. Facility was not available.

2. Arrange for audio-visual equipment.

Time: 10 minutes

Obstacles: Equipment was not available in-house. You now have to add a task to your list, 'Investigate equipment rentals.'

Saving time

What is the one major time saver you could use for the overall assignment that would save you about 50 per cent of your time? Should you:

a) Spend the necessary time planning the project?

b) Delegate most of the work to others?

c) Use a computer or word processor to record information?

These would all help. But there's something more important. What was the assignment? To set up your company's Annual Meeting. This means your company holds it every year. So find out who did it last year! Has the person left the company? There should be a company file identifying all the details of last year's project. Consider too, those tasks completed by co-workers or friends. Don't start projects from 'scratch' unless it's absolutely necessary.

Before planning any long-term assignment, try to determine how you can be 'lazy.' Being 'lazy,' is really using effective time management. Take five minutes before tackling long-term assignments to identify how you can cut corners or use work done by yourself or others in the past as a pattern. Stop re-inventing the wheel.

Procrastination

Are you forever dragging your heels, putting things off, being late? Procrastination is a serious work-place problem. It's such a serious matter that it's second in line as to why companies fire employees. (First in line are personality clashes between supervisors or co-workers). It also ends friendships both at work and in private life.

How can you tell when procrastination has become a serious problem?

- When you have something important to do, not much time to do it in, but find yourself looking for other diversions instead.
- When *you* set deadlines and don't meet them.
- When you constantly delay making important decisions.
- When you work furiously at the last minute to complete crucial assignments.

There are five basic kinds of procrastinators:

1. Last-minute type - They wait until the last minute and work around the clock to meet deadlines.

2. I'll decide later - They postpone decisions until events resolve the situation or they're forced to decide.

3. Perfectionists - They must complete all tasks faultlessly, no matter how small or insignificant. They need to learn how to discriminate in the importance they place on assignments.

4. I'll show you! - They delay assignments as a way of retaining a sense of personal power and control. (Watch for this sign in your staff or your children. They may use it to 'get back' at you).

5. Muddler - They put off work because of bad habits, poor organisation, trying to do too much or there's a lack of set procedures. They are the people who go around in ever-widening circles getting nowhere. They start an assignment and before it's completed, go onto another one. They seldom complete assignments on time.

When facing a distasteful task, promise yourself you'll give fifteen minutes of hard effort on it. You'll probably find that the momentum you've started will keep you going until you finish the task.

Others don't get tasks done simply because of disorganisation. They start tasks, but don't finish them; they rush right in at the beginning of the day without thinking about what they should be doing and when; or neglect the important step of determining what has priority and what doesn't.

Think for a moment of someone you know who's well organised. I'll bet you'll agree that they're effective time managers. So learning how to manage your time will help you do the things you want to do in your life. Try increasing your work pace from time to time. On the other hand, don't be a clock-watcher - tense about filling every minute. Recognise the value of time spent relaxing.

I was fortunate to be born with a high energy level. This can be an asset or a detriment. Instead of gearing my energies at a specific target, I found that I was going around in 'every widening circles' accomplishing little and often getting in the way of others who were more organised. Before I learned time management techniques, I had a tendency to start more than one assignment or task and move onto another before finishing the first one. It was normal for me to have several assignments on the go at one time, with very few finished at the end of a day. Then I learned how to set priorities and how important it was to spend my time on issues that were of high priority to me. This took diligent effort on my behalf to tackle one task at a time, but the rewards were many.

After I listed my priorities and had chosen the most important one, I could push the other assignments out of my mind. I knew my 'To Do' list would prompt me when I was ready to tackle the next task. No longer was I distracted with thoughts about my next assignment, while completing the first one. This way, I could focus my high energy on one task at a time. I learned that because other matters weren't distracting me, I could get much more done than I ever thought possible.

That's the secret - focusing your energy in one direction at a time, instead of letting it get scattered around. Consider time as money and invest it wisely. So focus, focus, focus.

Reward vs. punishment

If you have problems motivating yourself to get something done, try giving yourself a reward for completing the task. Behavioural science experts explain that: 'Any behaviour that's followed by something pleasant is inclined to be reinforced and is more likely to happen again. Punishing yourself for goofing-off is not nearly as effective as rewarding yourself for success.'

This reward could be as simple as giving yourself an extended break after completing a difficult assignment or as elaborate as arranging to go on your dream vacation.

Lateness:

There are three basic kinds of personalities relating to time management. Let's assume there was a meeting called for 10:00 am:

Type 1: This person arrives right at 10:00 am.
Type 2: This person arrives at 10:10 am and acts as if s/he's on time.

70

Type 3: This person arrives at 9:50 am and acts as if s/he's 'just made it!'

Those who arrive ten minutes late run into more problems than the early bird. What do you think runs through the minds of those who cared enough to be there on time? Those waiting probably felt that the latecomer thinks they aren't important. Otherwise, why would they act as if their time was more important than those waiting? This is a serious put-down that can cause repercussions for the latecomer.

The ones who worry unless they're early for everything; can waste valuable time. They should bring some short-term task they can complete in the ten minutes they're early for the appointment.

How to deal with professionals who keep you waiting

Have you ever seethed because a doctor, dentist, lawyer or other professional keeps you waiting for your appointment? Are patients becoming impatient or are professional people guilty of thinking their time is more valuable than everyone else's?

71

One man decided he'd had enough and billed his tardy doctor. When William Ennis sent his doctor a $90 bill for the hour he spent in the waiting room, he became a hero in North America. He received many calls from people - just thanking him for his courage.

What Ennis did was fight back. Although promptness was a recurring problem with his doctor, he'd done everything he thought possible to make sure he would see him promptly at 8:45 am. He'd also made it clear to the receptionist that he didn't want to wait. He even called ahead twice to confirm the time of his appointment.

After waiting an hour, Ennis vowed he wasn't going to take the doctor's lateness sitting down. So, he billed his doctor. When the doctor ignored the bill, he filed a lawsuit. The matter was settled out of court when the doctor agreed to donate the $90 to a community eye bank.

The Ennis' case was unusual. It was a visibly public battle, but it represents a quiet rebellion sweeping the country. Patients who have bucked the traditional waiting game say there are two reasons. They're more crunched for time and they've come to view doctors and other such professionals as simply business people and peers who should have the same time consideration for them. People have become less sheep-like and less in awe of professionals, so they're no longer accepting those inconveniences as a necessity of life. They're attacking the pocketbook of professionals. And it's working.

The bottom line is that a fifteen minute wait is okay - a half-hour or more wait that can't be blamed on an emergency, is unreasonable.

I can't say 'No!'

With your busy lifestyle, you probably have to manipulate your life to fit in all your responsibilities. Then something comes along that blows your plans. You find that people take advantage of you by coercing you into doing things you don't want to do. This can be a frustrating use of your time. Learn how to say *'No.'* Too many people feel guilty about saying *'No,'* but remember you're the master of yourself and have the freedom to choose how you spend your time and energies. Don't get involved in something you don't really want to do just because you couldn't say *'No.'*

Don't respond to requests or demands right away. Give yourself time to see if they really make sense. If you need to say *'No,'* don't feel guilty. Refuse additional requests or demands on your time by learning how to say *'No.'*

Do you find yourself saying *'Yes'* for any of the following reasons?

- You don't want to hurt someone's feelings.
- You don't want to explain why you want to say no.
- You don't want to say anything the other person might interpret as negative.
- You feel compelled to spend time with the person because you haven't seen him or her in months.
- The other person is particularly important to you.
- You would really like to oblige, but the timing is inappropriate.

74

Learning how to say 'no' when you want to, depends on increasing:

- Your self-respect.
- Your confidence about following your own standards and decisions.
- Your comfort about meeting your own personal needs.
- Your recognition that you aren't responsible for others' feelings.
- Your understanding that your worth does not depend on other people's judgements.
- Your comfort and confidence in pleasing yourself.
- Understanding that you can't please all the people, all the time.

How to say 'NO'

Try the following, should you have trouble saying *'no'* to any situation. Each step forward can help you learn when and how to say *'no'* comfortably.

Step 1: Pick one type of situation where you've said *'yes'* inappropriately several times during the past few months. Concentrate on this area first.

Step 2: Identify your reasons for saying *'Yes.'* Are you concerned that the answer *'no'* might injure the relationship? Are you worried about the other person's feelings?

Step 3: Put together a plan of action for preventing this next time. Mentally prepare yourself to say *'No.'*

Step 4: Practice your new response. Concentrate on how you sound and feel as you say *'No'* in a skilful and thoughtful way. Rehearse with an uninvolved person who has good judgement.

For example you've been willing to pick up a friend to take him to regularly planned meetings. You don't mind helping out, but are irked because he always keeps you waiting. The solution is to inform him of how frustrated you are by having to wait. Then explain that the next time you are to pick him up at 7:00 pm that you'll wait only until 7:05 pm and if he's not ready you'll leave without him. Be strong enough to follow-through with your plan.

Don't allow yourself to feel compelled to return a favour from a friend. Stop saying *'Yes'* to people because you believe *'No'* will hurt their feelings.

Time – Today's Silent Killer

CHAPTER THREE

Time management at work

In the business world I've heard the following complaints about time:

1. I have too much to do in my job.
2. Everyone wants everything now!
3. I have no time to do the things I really want to do.
4. Everything is done half-way, not the way I'd like them done.
5. I make mistakes because I hurry and it frustrates me.
6. I wish for once I could finish everything.
7. I want to advance my career, but don't have time to learn the things I require to advance to the next promotional level.
8. I'm sure my boss can't be pleased with my work - because I'm not!

Time 'leakage'

How much time do you lose through these 12 common time 'leaks?'

79

1. Starting a job before thinking it through. (Prepare 'To Do' Lists.)
2. Doing unproductive things from sheer habit. (Set priorities).
3. Keeping too many unnecessary records. (Clean out files on a regular basis).
4. Paying too much attention to low return on investment items. (Weed out the non-productive use of your time).
5. Failing to anticipate crises. (Use the 'A stitch in time saves nine' of preventive maintenance).
6. Making unnecessary visits or phone calls. (A poor time waster which can be deadly to your career).
7. Socialising for too long time between tasks. (Same as above).
8. Failing to build good barriers against interruptions. (Hold your phone calls and close your office door).
9. Doing things that should be delegated. (Let go of tasks - delegate).
10. Doing things that aren't part of the job. (Make sure you have an up-to-date job description).

11. Failing to plan regularly with your boss. (Set up regular meetings.)
12. Engaging in personal work before starting business work. (Set priorities and stick to them).

Bottlenecks:

Bottlenecks occur whenever a person fails to take essential action, because of indecision, laziness, mistaken priorities, stubbornness, overwork or because they procrastinate.

Supervisors can be bottlenecks when they don't delegate properly so their employees are always busy.

Here's an example of how to deal with one kind of bottleneck. You need to submit month-end reports and require information from people in other departments to complete them. One of the people is always late sending the necessary material to you. You have two choices in dealing with her.

1. Talk to her to identify the problems she's causing you. Start by saying, *'I have a problem and I need your help in solving it.'*

Then add: *'For the last three months, I've had to scramble to get my month end report ready. The problem is that I don't have the necessary information from you to complete my report. Is there anything you can do to make sure this doesn't happen in the future? I really need your co-operation on this.'*

2. If step one doesn't work, ask your supervisor to speak to the other person's supervisor so you can get the necessary information on time.

3. Or submit your report stating, 'Information from XYZ department was not available.'

Helping your staff set priorities

How much time does your staff spend determining what are priority As Bs etc.? Do they have to guess what you want done first? Try attaching coloured labels to the work you give them. For instance, you might use a red label for Urgent (require immediate attention), yellow (do today) and green (can wait until tomorrow). On the label, make sure you include date and time of day you need the task completed.

82

If you share an assistant, make sure you and the other supervisors keep in touch. Have an early morning meeting with them. Instruct your personal assistant to let you know if there is too much to do and help choose priorities by discussing work with the other supervisors.

Are you making the situation easier for your support staff or do you sabotage their success? Assistants suggest that you keep them informed by communicating with them regularly. Many supervisors keep their support staff 'in the dark' as a way of maintaining control. Not only do they maintain control but they isolate themselves from the people hired to help them do a good job.

- Tell your staff what you expect of them.
- Explain how they're doing and what's behind your e-mail.
- Why a particular e-mail is so important
- Where you're going and when you'll be back.

If a client makes a complaint about one of your staff, listen carefully. Then tell them, 'I'll get back to you when I've had an opportunity to investigate this matter.' Try to stay away from situations where you have to make a snap judgment without consulting your staff or giving them the chance to defend their actions.

Let your support staff do some decision-making, especially with routine matters when they know the answers. Have them answer routine e-mails for you. Give your personal assistant the authority to send routine letters on your behalf, leaving critical, sensitive or legal e-mails and letters for your attention. S/he'll gain confidence, feel more important and more a part of the team. Prepare before giving support staff instructions (consideration), don't change it all with an afterthought.

When you make appointments, keep them. Save your staff the embarrassment of having to make excuses for you. When clients or other senior people leave messages or request information, get back to them promptly, otherwise your staff are forced to make explanations for you.

Keep their work-flow consistent. Your assistant must see you early in the day so s/he can help you plan his/her day. Be sure you check your e-mails before sending them – you can't get them back if there are errors.

Make sure your assistants are aware of your deadlines and how much you need their help to reach them. Get their help with such tasks as; making sure files are ready and getting the necessary information for you - anything that will make for a smooth-running project.

Bring-forward file:

Rather than sift through paperwork three or four times, it's handy to have a Bring-forward file. This works for e-mails as well. A bring forward file is usually a pocket file with dates on each pocket or separate files with dates on them for follow-up. Use them to file information about tasks you want to do on specific days.

For instance, you called to speak to George and find he is out-of-town until Friday, the 6th. You would file the information in your BF file for Friday, with a note to remind you what you wanted to ask him. This way you won't forget to call him that particular day.

Is your in-basket out of control?

One of the few certainties of working life is a perpetually refilling in-basket whether it is on our desk or a raft of e-mails we face on our computer. As soon as you reach the bottom, it starts filling up again! Just when you think you've finally gained a grip on things, your control is shattered by catching a glimpse of your overflowing in-basket.

In part, we have progress to thank for this predicament. Technology promised us the paperless office and then promptly gave us faxes, photocopies, computer printouts and spreadsheets. Since we all have better assignments to do than look at every piece of paper the moment it crosses our path, we often wind up with teetering in-baskets. This can add to our personal stress and send a signal to higher-ups in the organisation that we're not on top of our work.

Is there nothing to do, then, but complain? The problem isn't too much paper or too little time. We don't use our in-baskets correctly in the first place. We substitute them for a daily paperwork system. Something lands on our desks and we put it in the in basket and leave it there until we get around to handling it. Eventually everything piles up. Instead, use the philosophy of - toss it, refer it to someone else, act on it or file it. Just don't leave it there.

Handle each paper only once after sorting. This means that if you can't deal with something until Friday, it goes into your bring-forward file for that date. Start a sorting system for your paperwork so, if you can't do something right away, you can keep it somewhere and take care of it later. (Not in your in-basket!) If you have to talk to someone about the information, put that item on your to do list or route the information directly to the individual with a note explaining what you want done with the material.

Keep in mind the 80/20 rule. Only 20% of what lands on your desk are 'A' priorities and at least 20% of it should be thrown away immediately. This is how you can set priorities with all the information from your in-basket and other sources:

1. Classify information into 4 piles - Priority As, Bs, Cs and Ds (I do the same with telephone messages and left over assignments from the day before).

   You should put your Ds in 'File 13' (your garbage can).

   Don't keep anything unless you really have a use for it. You could throw out 20% of your mail and not even miss it!

   Cancel unnecessary subscriptions.

   As the day progresses and new assignments come along, add them to your To Do list (slotting them between two other tasks)

   Update your list as new items come up during the day.

   I make my To Do list in pencil, so I can change a priority A5, to an A6 if necessary. Have one list - not scraps of paper. Remember, it's not crossing out items that counts, but making better use of your time.

Remember to check your BF (bring forward) file for that day. If you're sorting your mail on Monday and find that there's something you can't do until Friday, put it in your bring forward file for that day. This way, you're only dealing with that piece of paper once after sorting (one crucial time management rule).

2. Now that you have three piles - As, Bs & Cs. Determine whether you have enough time to complete your As. Do you have time to do any Bs as well? If so, add them to your list. If not, put these Bs in your bring forward file for later completion.

3. Find an empty folder and put all your Cs into it and put the file out of sight. Now you can deal exclusively with only the important and urgent items.

4. Make a To Do list of what you wish to accomplish that day. Update 'To Do' list throughout the day (including the time you estimate tasks will take) as you add new assignments.

5. Clear your work area of all unnecessary items. This is the secret for those who

always have a messy desk. When everything has its place and everything is in its place, time saving is an obvious asset.

6. Next determine which is your Priority A1, A2, A3, A4, etc. and try to identify the time each task will take to complete.

7. Remember to check your daytimer or calendar for appointments and deadlines.

8. Know your limitations. If you find that you can't do all your tasks that day, decide whether you can delegate any tasks to someone else. Keep your boss informed if you see that you can't finish something.

9. Don't start another project before you finish the first one.

10. Train yourself to focus all your attention on the task you're doing. If you're distracted by other assignment, the job you're doing will suffer. When the next job is on your To Do list, train yourself to forget about it until it's time to tackle that project.

11. Keep a red-coloured file that contains information relevant to phone calls you can expect to receive. If you leave a message for someone to call you, place a little

reminder note on the information to remind you of the questions you want to ask them. Keep this file near your telephone for easy access.

12. When you know you're likely to procrastinate when completing certain tasks, make sure you slot those tasks into your high energy time. When they're next on the list, self-discipline can make you 'get it over with' instead of putting it off unnecessarily.

13. Are there days when you wonder what you've been doing all day? Here's when your To Do lists prove their value. Just look at what you've checked off. It also proves to those who monitor your work, that you have completed your tasks. Remember that 80% of the value comes from 20% of your time, so put your time where the value is.

14. Make proper use of filing cabinets. When you finish a project, immediately file it out of the way. Filing cabinets can be a problem too. They often have too much out-dated material in them. Try to determine a discard date when you can

eliminate much of the material in each file - just keep the important information.

If you take a stab at desktop organisation and dutifully file everything away and can never find anything again - there's a good reason. You're probably a creative person. Creative people often function best with clutter around them. They need the sensory stimulation. If they try to conform to a system that deprives them of this, they can't do their best work. Still, there are ways for even the most clutter-driven types to keep notes, e-mails and other documents from getting out of control

One helicopter company employee uses humour to keep things in order. He keeps three baskets on his desk. One he labelled 'In.' One he labelled 'Out.' A third he labelled 'Hovering.'

Since creative people get bored with routines quicker, investing in a few gadgets might be the key. Try separating your piles and putting them in see-through plastic file boxes. They're still your piles, but now they'll appear more orderly. Multicoloured notepaper and oversize coloured paper clips can help turn tedious tasks into a game. As for the in-basket - give yourself permission to shuffle through it from time to time to pick out the important items. If you can find something in three minutes or less, you're fine. Files or piles, it doesn't matter, as long as you can find it.

If you're receiving work from more than one person, you might think, 'How can I keep multiple bosses happy when they say everything is a priority red?' The employee should take the stack of red labelled work to each boss and ask his or her co-operation in re-defining what is actually a red priority.

Working overtime

Do you find that overtime is a usual activity rather than the occasional occurrence that it should be? Do you find that you're so tired at the end of the day that it takes you twice the time to complete assignments? Try coming into work early (before the rest of the employees). That extra time at the beginning of the day will enable you to accomplish twice as much because of fewer interruptions. This is far better than trying to fit your work into the end of a stressful day (unless of course - you're not a morning person in the first place).

In most areas, when an employee works over a certain number of hours a week (most often 44 hours) overtime is paid. Their overtime is usually paid at time-and-a-half or even double time. Instead of making their staff work overtime when they're tired, employers would be wise to have someone else come in to do the overtime work. There are several reasons for this:

1. The part-time employee is 'fresh' and not tired after putting in a full-day's work.
3. It enables former employees who wish to work only part-time to keep their skills and knowledge of the company current. This enables former employees (often women with small children) to keep up-to-date on company practices and procedures.
4. A retired person can often provide the skills, wisdom and experience to fill-in for the shorter hours of work.

5. The company saves money on company benefits and by paying straight time rather than time-and-a-half. They'll also save money because they're paying the extra person only straight time instead of paying overtime to a tired employee.

Delegation

When delegating a task to anyone (whether it's to an employee, a child or a friend) you must give them both the responsibility to do the task and the authority necessary to get the job done. Here are some criteria you should know about delegation:

Responsibility: The actual tasks that require completion.

Authority: Having the authority necessary to make the decision and take the appropriate action. Consider these examples:

- An employee had the responsibility of ordering office supplies for his department, so he went to the supply depot to fill the order. He learned that he couldn't take the

95

supplies because he didn't have signing authority for his department.

- A supervisor asks a staff member to go to Human Resources Department to obtain a personnel file of an employee. They won't release the file because he doesn't have the authority to receive the confidential file.
- A staff member goes to a computer company to pick up a new computer monitor. They refuse to give it to him because he doesn't have a purchase order from the company.

These employees were delegated the responsibility to do the task, but lacked the authority to fulfil their obligations. What an unfortunate waste of the employees' time.

Accountability:

1. Delegated accountability:
   A task is delegated to an employee by the supervisor. The employee is accountable to supervisor for the task.
2. Final accountability:
   This stays with the supervisor (or parent) who delegated the task to the person.

Employees must understand that they're accountable to their supervisor but that the supervisor is ultimately responsible for what they do.

Where are you now?

How are you handling your work-load right now? The following will help you determine areas where improvement will help:

1. From memory - try to recap the duties you fulfilled yesterday (or your last working day. Write these down.)

2. For each of your duties - ask yourself the following questions:

   (a) What would have happened if you hadn't done the task?

   (b)   What could have happened if you'd left it until later?

   (c) Could someone else have done it? Who?

3. Did you attend to all 'Priority A' matters?

4. Did you feel comfortable that you had a productive day? Why?

5. Were there any bottlenecks that kept you from completing your tasks? What solutions would you suggest?

6. Are you subject to constant interruptions? How do you handle them? Is there a better way?

7. What do you feel you can do to follow-up on the above suggestions? (Start a To Do list to correct any of the above.)

Interruptions and crises

Do you get upset every time the phone rings? Do you find it difficult getting back to your original task? But phone calls can be as important (if not more important) than the task you were doing. Say to yourself, *'That's my job calling!'* Quickly get to the purpose of a telephone call and then recognise your need to return to other priority 'A' tasks. Productivity will increase. Frustration will decrease.

Get back on track after interruptions. Don't use interruptions as excuses to procrastinate. Don't complain or take a break. Ask staff interrupters to write their problems down including perceived solutions to their problems before approaching you for help.

Supervisors should keep an open-door policy so their staff feel confident coming to them when they need help. An employee's major function is to do a good job for the company and make their supervisor look good. Because a supervisor's main function is to help their employees do a good job, it's to the supervisor's advantage to be available when needed. However, this does not mean that they have to coddle their staff.

If supervisors have employees who are constantly interrupting them with trivial matters, they should answer their staff's questions with one of their own. Ask, *'What do you think you should do?'* Most employees know the best solution to their problem, but just want their supervisor's confirmation that they're right. Soon the employees' confidence in their own decision-making ability will make sure that they don't bother the senior official with trivial matters.

If interruptions are the norm for your day, you can start by separating the good interrupters from the bad ones. Good interrupters are those who convey information to you or want answers to important questions that only you can answer. Bad interrupters can be workers who refuse to accept responsibility and want to delegate upward. Others are those that are of low priority when you compare them with your existing priorities. Knowing the difference between the two and applying the systems on this page will help you regain control of interruptions.

Since interruptions have different purposes, you need to classify them and treat them differently. For instance:

How do you deal with idle chatting and non-productive complaining? Depending on your style and workplace atmosphere, you may want to inform others of your ground rules. One might be to have others think twice before interrupting you by asking themselves:

a) Have you stopped to think if you can answer this question without bothering me?
b) You may interrupt me if there is something you think I need to know right away or under one of the following conditions:

- You're genuinely stumped.

100

- You must make a decision that exceeds your authority.
- You have a personal problem that's affecting your work.
- You have an interpersonal problem with another worker that you've already tried at least twice to resolve.

Kinds of interruptions:

Quickly classify interruptions. It enables you to get the information you need and cuts time lost dealing with people who interrupt for no good purpose or at the wrong time. Using this system, you can group interruptions into four classes based on why and when they happen.

- The right question at the wrong time. A worker has an important question or problem - but arrives at your door when you're unable to devote enough time or attention to it.

Solution: Take a few moments to assure the worker that s/he has made you aware of a valuable piece of information - something you really needed to know. Let your attitude

101

convey your eagerness for further discussion and agree to a time to discuss the problem later.

- The wrong question at the right time. Just because you have a quiet moment is no reason for you to take part in a decision that a worker could make for him or herself.

Solution: If you see that a worker is attempting upward delegation, don't be tempted, even if you do have time to devote to it.

- The wrong question at the wrong time. When a worker interrupts your busy day with an unnecessary question, it's time to let them know you're displeased. Don't, however, just get angry, since that's not instructive and won't cause the worker to improve.

Solution: Underscore your policy about interruptions.

- The right question at the right time. What about the staffer who asks the right question

102

at the right time? That's an activity to reward. Your staffer has shown judgement and tact.

Solution: Encourage more of such activity with statements like, *'I'm glad you brought me up to speed on this at once,'* or, *'Good idea.'* Encouraging excellent judgement will have a greater benefit on departmental operations and will discourage the bad.

How to prevent interruptions

Be less accessible to drop-in visitors by re-organising your work area. Don't have too many chairs in the room or place them too close to your desk. Have a clock in a prominent place for easy referral. Also:

a) Keep a log to determine when, how long and who causes your interruptions.
b) If the person wants to chat, suggest they catch you at coffee break.
c) Set time limits - and stick to them.
d) Meet others in their office, so you can leave when you wish or

103

e) Meet visitors in a conference room, reception area or in the hall if you want the meeting to be short and there's no need for privacy.

f) If receptionists' desks are of average height, they might feel the need to chat with those waiting for appointments. Solve this problem by installing desks with a higher front. This allows them to continue working, without having the guilty feeling that they're being rude to office visitors. This still allows them to see over the top of the barricade to check what visitors are doing and to watch the waiting room.

Handle interruptions by setting a time limit and sticking to it. Say, *'I don't have a minute; but I do have five.'* Then start timing. After five minutes, tell the person you have to get back to your original project. Set the stage in advance. Let them know you're really busy! Don't be rude, but keep them informed about your time crunch.

If you're writing a report, keep a pen in your hand or fingers on the keyboard. If a person drops into your office, stay standing. If they sit down on a chair in your office, sit on your desk.

Avoid small talk when you're busy. Small talk makes large interruptions out of what could be small ones. Try not to feel annoyed. Give interrupters undivided attention. Listen carefully. Don't interrupt and don't let your mind drift - it's time-consuming. Help them get to the point. You might ask, *'What do you wish to discuss?'* or *'What can I do for you today?'* Don't be afraid to say *'no'* if they ask for too much (even your boss). If the meeting drags on and you have accomplished what you need, tell them you have another appointment now. Stand up, hold out your hand and ease them towards the door.

Train customers or co-workers to leave detailed messages in your voice mail or send you e-mails. Then you can have the answers ready when you call back or return the e-mail.

If you can't help them now, don't let them go away empty handed. Learn to say *'no'* graciously. Recognise that it is better to say 'no' at the start than disappoint people because you're over-committed. Or promise to do what they want later. Explain that you're working on other assignments or tell them who else they might ask to help out. Or you might ask, *'Could we continue this, when I'm not so busy?'*

When possible have someone else take your telephone calls. In urgent situations, remove yourself by going to a conference room or other neutral zone.

How to control crises situations

Anticipate known deadlines and potential crises. Don't put tasks off to the last minute. Make contingency plans. Cross-train your staff so if one is away, another can take over. Watch that you don't lose your cool. That just makes matters worse and can alienate others.

Concentrate on solving the problem instead of giving blame to why the problem or crisis occurred. Don't make matters worse, by forgetting good time management. Use your 'fight or flight' energy to find solutions instead of yelling and blaming others. Spend your energy on finding a plan of action that will work. Recognise that this is just part of a normal day - not a catastrophe. It's also an opportunity to use your creative juices to come up with innovative solutions to the problem.

Solutions to time wasters:

Improper use of time by yourself or others causes many problems. Here are some suggestions:

1. Telephone interruptions:

While telephones can be essential lifelines of business, they also can waste a lot of time. An interruption by telephone calls can be distracting and disrupt our flow of concentration when we're working on an important project. It's useful to keep a three-minute timer by the phone to lessen the social aspects of the call. Be careful you're not too abrupt. Other steps to take are:

a) Schedule all calls for a certain time of day.
b) Differentiate between business and personal calls.
c) Keep business calls to business matters.

d) Set a time limit to conversations.

e) List the issues you wish to discuss when making phone calls. Many people encourage chatting. How you respond to someone who's showing signs that they want to chat, will determine the outcome of the conversation.

For example: A regular client phones in and enquires, *'Hi Merle, did you have a nice long week-end?'* They can hook you with this kind of question and you'll probably spend the next fifteen minutes discussing your respective weekends. On the other hand, you could reply, *'It was great, Merle. What can I do for you today?'*

You've steered the conversation right back to the topic. If you feel this is being too abrupt, you might say, *'It was great, Merle. I wish I had time to tell you about it, but I'm swamped. What can I do for you today?'*

2. Drop-in visitors:

Sometimes, we have a need to socialise at the office, but we must be realistic when this becomes detrimental to our effectiveness. Try to encourage others to come to the point. Find a polite way of getting people who ramble, back on track. One way of doing this is to ask concise questions until you get the information. Other solutions are:

a) Distinguish business and personal visitors and treat accordingly.
b) (b) Have receptionist screen visitors before they see you.
c) (c) Discourage socialising - continue with your work.
d) (d) Be honest with visitors and state for instance, *'I've only got a few minutes - how can I help you.'* - and stick to it!

3. Meetings:

Meetings are held for a variety of reasons - legitimate business, to issue information, to provide an audience for someone, to socialise or simply out of habit. Other meetings are held by people who wish to pass the buck and get others to do tasks they should be doing. Some meetings outlast their original intent and become time wasters.

When preparing for a meeting, be clear about the goals you wish to reach. Give the participants a written agenda ahead of time, so they know what issues you'll be covering and can come prepared. Set time limits and stick to both the agenda and the time limitations.

If you're a supervisor, have regular morning meetings with your assistant to go over your respective To Do lists. When attending meetings, ask yourself, 'Is this meeting really necessary?' Be sure your attendance serves a purpose. Learn the purpose and objectives for a meeting and come prepared with related information. If you call a meeting, prepare a written agenda and distribute it in advance to give attendees time to prepare for the meeting. Then, stick to the agenda.

4. Ineffective delegation:

If you're a supervisor, avoid the tendency to 'Do it yourself.' Instead, think before acting and delegate. Never put off for tomorrow, what you can get someone else to do today. Is there anyone else in the organisation who could

110

perform the task, attend the meeting or travel to the convention? Improve your follow-up when you delegate tasks. Your job description as a supervisor includes consideration, confidence and communication with your staff. Spend more time training subordinates to do a better job. Select the best time of day to do the type of work. Improve your follow-up on delegated tasks.

If you're in a support position:

a) Talk with your manager to see if someone else can handle a duty that you feel doesn't fit your position.

b) Use paraphrasing to make sure you understand what your supervisor expects from you.

c) Ask for written instructions.

d) Have magazines and articles routed to others in the department. Have others circle any interesting article in the Table of Contents. When you receive the magazine back, you'll already know which articles are worth reading.

111

5. Lack of objectives/priorities and planning:

a) Ask for an up-to-date job description that includes standards of performance.
b) Define priority items.
c) Make 'To Do' lists and follow them.

6. Dealing with crisis situations:

a) Assess how often it happens.
b) Determine how you can stop future crisis (preventive maintenance).
c) Allow time for 'fighting fires' every day.
d) Don't put off or procrastinate (which can start a crisis situation).

7. Attempting too much at once:

a) Set objectives and priorities
b) Make daily To Do lists
c) Know when to say *'No'* to additional duties

8. Cluttered desk - personal disorganisation:

a) Allow time to organise. It will save time later
b) Reduce paperwork
c) Use verbal communication as often as possible

d) Put away anything you're not working on at present.

e) Return everything promptly to its place.

9. Inability to say *'No'*:

(See Chapter 2 for more information on this).

a) Take an assertiveness training course.

b) Realise that you can't please all the people all the time.

c) Recognise traps, manipulative games which can 'con' you into doing things you don't want to do.

d) Offer alternative solutions.

e) Decide the consequences should you say *'Yes.'*

f) Don't feel you have to explain your reasons for saying *'No.'*

g) Count to ten before saying *'Yes.'*

h) Realise that it's better to do **less** well, than **more**, poorly

10. Unclear communication - instruction:

a) Develop listening skills.

b) Practice paraphrasing and feedback.

c) Repeat instructions.

11. Confused responsibility and authority:

a) Have up-to-date job description.

b) Determine your level of responsibility and make sure you have the authority to carry out your responsibilities.

c) Determine your subordinates' level of responsibility and authority

12. Delayed, inaccurate information:

a) Check information source - don't listen to grapevine

b) Identify and deal with bottleneck employees

c) Practice listening skills

d) Use paraphrasing and feedback

13. Lack of self-discipline:

a) Keep a daily To Do list.

b) Set objectives and plan daily.

c) Set priorities and stick to them.

d) Schedule unpleasant tasks *first*.

14. Leaving tasks unfinished:

(a) Same as #13.

15. Untrained, inadequate staff:

a) Use 'old Timers' in your department to train new staff.
b) Ask for training for both you and your staff where required.
c) Know where to find company policy manuals; read and update them regularly.
d) Keep an information file of techniques you've learned for future use.
e) Spend more time training subordinates to do a better job.
f) Ask your assistant, *'How can we improve?'*

16. Socialising:

a) Control the urge.
b) Keep your socialising to coffee and lunch breaks.
c) Keep busy!

17. Indecision - procrastination:

a) Take an assertiveness training course.
b) Daily 'To Do' lists will keep you on track.
c) Ask others to help you determine when you're being indecisive or showing procrastination.
d) Have faith that you have the ability to do the job.

Time – Today's Silent Killer

CHAPTER FOUR

Time management at home

Introducing business to home management

Life runs smoothly at the office - but why does it fall apart at home? Where's the gas bill? When is Sally's next dentist appointment? What groceries do I have to pick up on my way home from work?

When you have a dual lifestyle (balancing a career and home duties) it's usually the home front that does you in. Learn to use business techniques in the home as well.

Planning is essential in getting your homemaking chores under control. Use lists for everything; groceries, chores that need doing around the house and yard (and who is expected to do them!) Also learn to set priorities. Is it more important to have a spotless house or to spend an hour teaching Sally how to knit or Johnnie how to fix his bike? Know what's important to you and what you can let slide when more important priorities come along. Your lists should be divided into:

Have to: (Priority As)
Need to: (Priority Bs)
Hope to: (Priority Cs)

Do you find that the daily pressures of work and home responsibilities leave you little time for you to spend just socialising or having private time? You need to find time for yourself. This area is usually low on the list of priorities for many, but in reality it should be near the top of the list. Unless you feel good about yourself and what you're doing, you'll be sacrificing your priorities for others, instead of putting your wishes first.

Wise parents learn that they must learn to be 'selfish' and do special things for themselves too. In turn, they'll be more effective when they're dealing with other parts of their lives. Putting yourself number one is not a sin - it's a necessity (providing you don't take it to excess and become purely self-centred).

Delegate jobs to your family and follow up. Follow-up to make sure that they've completed the task properly, give them training so they can improve the quality of their performance and give praise for a job well done. Decide what you'll do, if they don't complete their tasks. Be consistent with discipline and fair to all members of your family.

When you're cooking, make multiple batches. It doesn't take much longer to make meals for four days than one. Use your freezer as much as possible and freeze the extra three days' meals. Stop wasting your time picking up groceries every second day. Make fewer trips.

Some leave most of the family chores until the weekend, but find that their family doesn't have time to do activities together. To correct this, do your shopping Thursday evening instead of Saturday. Then, instead of waiting until Saturday to do your laundry (which ties you to your home unless you do all the batches at a Laundromat) pop a batch of dirty laundry into the washer as soon as you get home from work. While you're fixing dinner or mowing the lawn, the clothes are washed. Just before serving dinner, switch the clothes to your dryer. After your meal, fold the clothing. Do a batch of wash every day to keep on top of the chore.

For those jobs that pile up (like cutting the grass, painting the fence, shovelling the driveway, helping with spring cleaning) consider hiring a student to help you out.

How to organise yourself for work

One essential ingredient for men and woman who successfully juggle two demanding roles is Organisation. You must be organised; you just can't hope it will happen.

1. Plan your time: First decide what the important issues are. Some helpful tips are:

- If you find you're constantly late, set your watch 10 minutes ahead and pretend it's right.
- Prepare for the next day by choosing the outfit and accessories you'll be wearing in the morning. Pack your lunch the night before.

- If you tend to procrastinate and put things off - set yourself written deadlines and ensure you meet them!
- Try to have your family's appointments with dentists, physicians, music lessons etc. within walking distance of home, so older children can go without you.
- Use waiting time properly. Bring letters and reading material with you when you're on the bus or train or if you know you'll have to wait for others. While watching TV, sort out your tool box, do hand mending, sort the laundry, fix the cord on a kettle or do the ironing. Just don't waste that time.
- Get up an hour before everyone else. The bathroom is free and you can make a good start on housework, lunch packing, making a grocery list, polishing the car or watering the lawn.
- Let your fingers do the walking. Phone ahead to make sure the item you need is available.
- Do banking on-line or at an instant teller whenever possible. Pay bills there too.

2. Organise your home:

- Make sure each member of your family has written lists of chores you expect them to do and enforce this list. List chores they must complete on the weekend.
- Buy non-perishable foods in bulk. Try to shop only once a week.
- Keep lists; a grocery list on the fridge that everyone in the family adds to when something is running short.
- Keep paper and pencil by the phone for messages. Have a special place where you keep messages.
- When house cleaning, carry a bag with furniture polish, dust rag, garbage bag etc. with you to save steps.
- Keep non-productive phone calls to a minimum. Discourage drop-in visitors if you have a busy day; explain you're busy.
- Have them tag along while you work if necessary.
- Make full use of convenience foods and appliances (microwave ovens).

3. Clothing:

- Make a list of your existing clothing and note what's missing. Take a little swatch from a seam and carry it with you. You won't buy the wrong colour - it will match your existing wardrobe.
- Avoid purchasing hard-to-keep clothing - keep dry cleanable items to a minimum. Watch for dry cleaning specials for the remainder.
- In the summer, consider hiring a 'mother's helper' so they can take care of the babysitting and home care too. Screen applicants for this position carefully - choose the person who has a genuine liking for children and does a good job around the home. Ask questions about how they would deal with emergencies. Do your homework and have emergency phone numbers ready for your substitute parent. This arrangement will eliminate the need for alternative childcare if one of them catch a communicable disease and be refused at their usual day care centre.

Finding the right child care

A mother decides to go back to work, either because she wants to or because it's financially necessary. Though excited about the prospect of returning to work, she's anxious about the contradictory feelings of going back to work versus staying home with her children. How is she going to find time to look after all her home responsibilities?

Who will take care of the children while she's away? The thought of searching for someone else to care for her children gives her cold shivers. She recalls all the horror stories in the newspaper about abusive babysitters and child molesters.

Others worry that many nannies and babysitters are from other cultures, which could complicate the upbringing of their children. What these women are really looking for, are replacements for themselves, so they're not likely to find the exact match for their needs. Some compromises must be made, but never at the risk of the children's safety and well-being.

124

She'll need to check references of child-care workers and listen to her initial instincts about the person. After all, children are a couples' most precious legacy to the future. Even if the feelings about the child care worker are good, she'll still need to check references. If anything is questionable, she should listen to her instincts and look elsewhere. Unfortunately, many parents don't listen to their instinctive responses and serious problems are the result.

Obtaining help at home

Call a family conference whenever there's an important issue that involves the entire family. This could be when Mom goes back to work or when Dad gets a promotion and the family needs to move to another city. Have a meeting when a relative is very ill and may die or any other important family issue.

Leave 'chore' lists for your children for tasks you expect them to do during the day while you're at work. Make them feel part of a team - that they're contributing something valuable to the family unit. Plan special treats to reward good performance.

125

You may have scoffed at the above suggestion - because your children do little, if anything, to help out around the home. If you're working at a job away from the home (mothers and fathers too) it's time for your children to pull their load and do their share of the chores around the home. Hold family conferences to discuss problems within the family and to delegate new responsibilities. You also can use these conferences to touch base with how family members are doing towards completing tasks and activities.

To prepare for a family conference on delegation of tasks, the parents write down all the chores they need completed around the home and yard (include everything). Make a copy for each member of the family who's old enough to read. At the family conference:

1. Discuss the chores with your family and explain that because you work all day, you need their help in completing all the chores on the list.

2. Have each member look over the list and ask them to volunteer (yes volunteer!) for

126

certain chores. Have them make a commitment to you that they will do the chores they've chosen. Don't eliminate children 'because they're too young' - even a two-year-old can do the following chores:

a. put his or her dirty clothes in the clothes hamper

b. put his or her toys away when required

c. help with the dusting

d. make shelves neat (your plastic dishes, pots and pans)

e. arrange shoes in a closet

3. Delegate the leftover chores to the applicable person. Again, get their commitment that they'll complete the chores and you're depending on them to do their assigned chores.

Explain to your children that once they've made a commitment to you, that you won't nag them to do their chores, but will expect them to live up to their promises. Be sure to give positive feedback when you see they've done a job well. To make sure this process works, make sure you give rewards, signs of love and appreciation. Acknowledge jobs well done and arrange special family treats for exceptional work or anything above and beyond the call of duty.

Make sure they've received the necessary training to carry out their delegated duties. Pretend they're a subordinate at work and you're training them how to do a task. Set standards of performance, so they know exactly what you expect from them. Your idea of 'clean' might differ widely from their description. Confirm that your spouse does his or her equal share.

If you've received the excuse, *'I don't have time,'* help them plan their time. Try to avoid power struggles. If one teenager or child has the job of taking out the garbage, another cleans the bathroom (including the toilet) while another mows the lawn. Start job rotation to guarantee completion of distasteful chores. As a last resort, cut allowances and pay a neighbour's child to do the chores your children won't do.

One woman complained, *'My children have a lazy streak in them, but then, so does my husband. They keep putting off chores until I end up doing them myself.'*

Have a family conference, and then do what supervisors do in the workplace - find their hot button and push it. Some motivators that can encourage them to do their share are: money, extra benefits or privileges, better working conditions or the work itself (different chores). Giving them a sense of security is another motivator. Removal of security works well. This would involve removal of allowances or privileges. For instance, a mother who has to clean up her children's mess when she arrives home from work, could state that they're responsible for preparing their own dinner because she's busy cleaning up their mess.

In business, a good motivator is competition and challenge. The best motivator of all, however, are awards, praise and recognition of a job well done.

Start by explaining exactly what you expect of them (in writing, so they can refer to your instructions) then give them ample opportunity to improve their performance. If they refuse to conform, explain the consequences, if they fail again (you choose what happens - discipline or withdrawal of privileges).

In many families, a unique problem is surfacing. When grown children leave home, we assume that they'll stay away, eventually get married and carry on with their lives. With the economic downturn, however, many of these grown children have returned to the safety of their parents' homes. In addition to having extra mouths to feed and tend for, parents revert to old supervisory roles. Adult children expect all the privileges they had as children. A conscious effort and frank discussion are necessary if two generations of adults are to live together harmoniously.

All sorts of new situations will arise. For example: where it was not acceptable earlier for a parent to consider allowing children conjugal rights with a partner, now their grown children may want and expect this privilege.

In the middle

Often adults in their forties, who are still responsible for growing children, find they have the added responsibility for aging parents as well. These middle caregivers might feel pulled at both ends by the needs of their children, their work, their home responsibilities and their parents. They may wonder when they'll have time to spend on activities they want to do themselves. We're seeing three-generational family conferences becoming more prevalent.

In other families, by the time their children have grown, the parents can spend more time, energy and effort on not only their own needs, but those of their parents. The change in roles - children looking after parents and parents becoming dependent on children, is a transition for all involved. Suddenly the parental support the grown children had expected to last a lifetime and had counted on has disappeared. Some feel as if life has cheated them and they feel adrift in life for the first time.

Women do most of the looking-after of elderly parents regardless of whether they're their own parents or their spouses'. Most have full-time jobs and children of their own. As the demands increase, the part of their life that suffers most is their fun time with friends, their children and their spouses. It also can have a heavy financial toll if the woman has to give up her full- or part-time job to become a parent's caregiver. This continues, even when the burden of the 'hands-on-care' is over and the parent is in a nursing home. She continues to be the parents' watchdog, is defender of their rights and protector of their wellbeing. Men are encouraged to give more support with aging parents.

Grandparents too, have had to adjust to the shift in traditional roles. They now face family units made up of children, step-children, parents and step-parents and all the problems that go with those relationships. Because forty per cent of marriages end in divorce, the role of grandparents is changing. Some grandparents lose contact with their grandchildren when one parent moves away or an estranged in-law won't let grandparents have access to the children.

Other grandparents find the opposite and find themselves back in the parenting roll they felt was over when their children grew up. These grandparents find themselves in the middle of the dropping-off-and-picking-up routine when the custodial parent needs economical day care or after-school tending of their children. In many cultures, extended families are the norm and grandparents provide this care, whether the parents are divorced or together. However, in most of North American society, this just isn't an option, because of the distance between grandparents, their children and grandchildren. The need for effective time management is paramount in all the above family mixes.

How to give your family 'loving time'

Parents face common challenges: How to make the most of the time they have with their children, when time is a premium? And how can they make sure their children get the love and attention they need when parents are away from home eight hours plus a day?

These are questions most parents can't even ask their own parents, who probably never had to answer them. Both parents must find time for the following:

- Spend individual time with each child where they can have 'special' time with each parent. This can be 10 to 15 minutes each day and a set time on the weekend.

- Keep track of your children's 'other lives' - at the babysitter, the day care, kindergarten, school, sports and artistic activities. Learn about special events at school and take time to attend. Make it the responsibility of your children to keep you informed.

- Practice effective listening - try not to be judgmental. Don't make contact times with your children an inquisition. 'Hear' what your children are not saying - watch their body language.

- Drop unnecessary steps to complete tasks that will give you more time with your family. Prioritise activities, remembering that your children should hold a high priority for your home time.

- Enlist children's help or ask for their presence when you're doing chores, so you can 'chat.' Parents could converse with their children while changing the oil in their car and encourage the child to hand the necessary tools to them. Or other children could help bring items out of the refrigerator and help make a salad while they talk to their parent.
- Plan special outings that fit individual needs. At a family conference, have each member state the special activities they like to do as a family. Use this list when planning special outings.

At one time, I wanted to reward my children because of all the hard work they'd done to help me with chores. Many times (without being told) they pitched in and simply did the tasks. I wanted to reward them and tried to think of a reward they deserved.

They had never seen a theatre production with live actors before, so (even though the tickets were very expensive) I decided to buy tickets. Thank goodness, I consulted them before doing so. When asked what they'd like for a treat for all their hard work, they surprised me by suggesting that we go on a picnic to one of their favourite spots. I learned a lesson that day. What I thought was a reward for them, was not what they would have chosen for themselves. So ask them what they would prefer, rather than choosing the reward yourself.

- Learn to be aware of your stress level - don't over-react to minor incidences with your children. If you've had a bad day, explain this to your children and ask if you can talk to them later. Don't put them off too long - do follow-up on things they need to discuss with you.

- Don't feel guilty when you need 'private time.' Honour your children's need for privacy too. If you come home from work tired out, rather than brushing by your children without comment, admit to them that you've 'had a bad day.' Explain to them that you need a few minutes alone to, 'get your act together.' This is important, because children often assume that you're mad at them, rather than just tired from a hard day at work. You may find that they copy your actions when they've had a hard day too. Rather than snap at you they'll say, 'I need some time out Mom. I'll talk to you later about this.'

Are you a night or morning person?

Does it matter when your high-energy time is during the day? Yes it does. It affects everything you do. For instance, if you're the sort that needs three cups of coffee and it's 10:00 am before you really feel alive, then you're going to be in trouble at a 9:00 am meeting. However, at 7:00 pm, you're probably raring to go.

You probably already know where you fit, but the following questionnaire might enlighten you more:

1. What time do you feel best about getting up?
   (5) 5 to 6:30 am.
   (4) 6:30 to 7:45 am.
   (3) 7:45 to 9:45 am.

(2) 9:45 to 11 am.

(1) 11 am to noon

2. How easy is it for you to get up in the morning?

(1) Not at all easy

(2) Not very easy

(3) Fairly easy

(4) Very easy

3. How tired do you feel the first hour after waking up?

(1) Very tired

(2) Fairly tired

(3) Fairly refreshed

(4) Very refreshed

4. You have a meeting tomorrow. What time do you think you'll give your best performance?

(6) From 8 to 10 am.

(4) 10 am to 1 pm.

(2) 1 to 5 pm.

(0) 7 to 9 pm.

5. One night you must remain awake between midnight and 4 a.m. for a work assignment. You have no commitments the next day.

Which alternative suits you best? (Choose only one).

(1) You would not go to bed until after the watch is over

(2) You would take a nap before and sleep after

(3) You would sleep before and nap after

(4) You would take all sleep before the watch

6. A friend invites you to jog with him. He jogs between 7 and 8 am. How do you think you would perform?

(4) Well

(3) Reasonably well

(2) Would find it difficult

(1) Would find it very difficult

7. If you have to wake up at a specific time every morning, how dependent are you on an alarm clock?

(4) Not at all

(3) Slightly

(2) Fairly dependent

(1) Very dependent

8. At what time in the evening do you feel tired and need sleep:

(5) 8 to 9 pm.
(4) 9 to 10:30 pm.
(3) 10:30 to 12:00 am.
(2) 12:00 to 2 am.
(1) 2 to 3 am.

Add up the scores for each answer. The higher the score, the more likely you are to be a morning person. A score of 22 is halfway between morning and night lark.

The hurry-up epidemic

In the past 50 years, our culture has sped up at an accelerating rate. If someone was transplanted from the 60's to the present, they'd be amazed at how fast things go, from the speed of our cars, to the pace of our movies.

People used to operate on the yearly, monthly and daily cycles of the sun and the moon, tides and seasons. Increasingly, we're living in a new, artificial kind of time that clicks by at the lightening-fast pace of computers. While the most basic human time reference is 60 seconds, a computer operates in nanoseconds - and one-billionth of a second is a unit of time beyond our ability to experience. Snapping your fingers - once the symbol of instant response - takes 500 million nanoseconds!

All the high-tech devices that were to give us more free time have had the opposite effect. One need never be further out of touch with our offices than the nearest phone or computer. Many people find it impossible to escape, no matter where they are. In the past decade, the average person's work-week has skyrocketed from an average of 40 hours to 48 hours. We're actually getting back very little from our high-speed gadgets - and we're losing our humanity in the process.

How to 'hang loose'

Tired of feeling trapped in a race against time? Time sickness can be cured. Coping with it can be as simple as sitting back in your chair or as involved as biofeedback, hypnosis or meditation. These techniques will help you slow down as well as become more productive.

Reset your inner clock. Does 15 minutes sometimes feel like 15 seconds? Individuals on

141

the fast-track often have an accelerated sense of time because of the pressure to get tasks done - that only adds to their stress level. However, you could change your perception of time.

Take a time out. The first time-technique many therapists recommend to a time-sick person is to sit quietly for 10 - 15 minutes, four times a week. If you're at home, turn off the television or radio, turn on the answering machine and dim the lights. If you're at the office, close the door and have your calls held. Day One will be the hardest. Those 15 minutes will feel like an hour, but the more you do it the easier it will become. I call these 'mental health breaks.'

Set your priorities. Family is, friends are and perhaps only some parts of your job are priorities. Decide what is possible to accomplish, then be ruthless with time bandits. Shorten endless calls or unimportant office visits, with a polite *'Thank you for calling,'* or *'I have to prepare for a meeting now.'*

142

Find small ways to get back in touch with the natural flow of time. Ditch the digital watch because all you have are numbers screaming, *'Do it now!'*

Adjust your schedule to fit your personality type. Not everyone would be happy dropping out or moving to Hawaii or the Mediterranean. Nevertheless, most of us are more efficient when we take time off occasionally to refuel. Learn to put everything into perspective.

Time – Today's Silent Killer

CHAPTER FIVE

The importance of goal setting

Where do you want to go?

A goal is a dream with a time frame. It's an effective method of planning for the future and gives life direction and a destination. It's important to write down your goals, so you can refer to them and can tell when you've reached them. Start by setting realistic, written goals.

It's unusual how some people spend their goal-setting energies only on pleasurable activities. For instance, they'll save for years for a trip to the Mediterranean yet won't spend one minute finding out what job would be the best for them. This doesn't make much sense considering that they'll be spending about ten hours a day, five days a week either getting ready for, travelling to or working for most of their adult lives.

Unless you participate in personal goal setting, you'll be missing out on one of the great highs in life. Mainly, we set goals to better ourselves

145

or to reach a higher station in life. Many people set goals too low or give themselves escape clauses and wonder why they accomplish so little.

We can change all this by setting concrete goals for ourselves and writing them down. Goals are statements of measurable results we want to achieve. They provide a means for translating wishes into reality. They help people know when they've achieved or won and provide a basis for determining where to concentrate their effort in the future.

How often should you set goals? As often as necessary. Goal setting, whether it is a career or lifetime goal is an ongoing activity. As we set one goal, it's necessary to have another simmering on the 'back burner' that we can sink our teeth into as soon as we reach our earlier goal. Otherwise, you're likely to have a 'downer' when you reach your original goal.

Think about the last time you made plans for a special holiday. Remember the plans you made and how it became a large part of your life until it happened? Do you remember too, that when you came back, you felt somehow empty? This empty feeling would not have occurred if you'd prepared by having something exciting to return to. You could have planned a party with your friends to share the photographs you took on your vacation. Or before you went on your trip, you started working towards other goals.

Should you only work on one goal at a time? No - you can work towards several at one time, possibly one in each quadrant of your life - personal, family and career.

Lifetime and career goals

To be completely successful, set your goals in several facets of your life. You'll want to make personal, family, social, financial, spiritual, community and career goals. Here are examples of lifetime and career goals.

Lifetime goal: By the time I reach 30 years of age, I'll marry, have two children and be employed as a professional engineer.

147

Career goal: Before December of this year I'll become Assistant Buyer for my firm (a short-term career goal). Within five years I'll become Merchandising Manager for a clothing firm (a long-term goal).

The importance of setting goals

As I mentioned earlier, it's important that you channel you life in the direction you wish it to go. If you simply put your head down and do your work, you'll often lose track of what is really important in life. With our busy lifestyles, it's easy to continue doing what we've been doing and 'go with the flow.' Some people float through life without setting goals and drift into situations almost by accident. Some find themselves in a rut, but don't know how to get out of it. Others waste their talents and abilities waiting for 'something to happen.' Don't wait for something to happen - make it happen! Accomplish this with serious goal setting.

It's amazing how many people never spend time determining what they want out of life, nor how they intend to reach their goals. If you're already a goal setter, you may be ready for a reminder that goal setting is a life-time activity.

Think about the successful people you know. Did they put a lot of time, energy, effort and dedication into getting where they wanted to go? You'll probably find that they did, because success doesn't come without all of those attributes. You have to be willing to put out that energy. We're only on this merry-go-round once, so why not ride your favourite coloured horse?

Types of goals

Positive/negative goals

It's important that your goals are positive rather than negative. It's easier to start doing something, than to stop doing something you don't want to do. For instance, a positive goal could be: *'I'll budget my income better so that I can use it to ...'* Rather than a negative goal: *'I'll stop wasting money on unnecessary expenses.'*

149

Short and long-term goals

Goals can be short or long term. A short-term goal can take one day, one week or possibly up to six months to complete. It's usually part of a long-term goal which can take from six months to ten years or more. Long term goals are harder to realise, so if possible break them down into shorter, more easily managed goals.

Tangible and intangible goals

Then there are tangible and intangible goals. Tangible goals are those that relate to something you can see and touch. Intangible goals relate to behaviour and attitudes and are harder to achieve than tangible goals.

Framing my goals so they're attainable

Just stating your goals is not enough. Your goals must be clear and attainable. Here are some examples of good and bad lifetime goals:

1. **To improve my tennis game by June 1st, 20__, at a cost not to exceed $150.00.**
   For practical purposes this may be okay, since presumably the only one who needs to know, is the one affected. From a purely

goal setting standpoint however, this is weak. What does 'improve' mean? Is it related to serve, backhand, volley, foot work or all of these? If not identified in the goal itself, the specific results should be part of the action plan. This could be as simple as meeting the approval of your instructor or your tennis partner. One of the expense factors to consider would be the amount of time you'll be committing.

So your re-written goal would be:

Suggested: To win the approval of my tennis partner for my court performance by June 1st, 20__, with an investment of five practice hours per week and an out of pocket expenses not to exceed $150.00.

2. To give up smoking.

Obviously, you will need a target date at the very least. That may be all you need to add if you plan to do it 'cold turkey.' Otherwise, if you plan to taper down or introduce some compensating activities, your action plan becomes critical. You won't require cost factors unless you plan to enrol in a group or incur some other directly-related expense. However, as a strong incentive to quit, you could use the savings you'll derive by not buying cigarettes to buy something special for yourself.

Suggested: To give up smoking by September 1st, 20__. Action plan: Reduce to one pack per day by July 2nd: half a pack per day by August 1st: five cigarettes per day by August 15th: and none by September 1st, 20___.

3. **To read one novel a month for the next 12 months,** five hours a week, at a cost not to exceed $100.00.

   This goal statement is okay. Set up a simple chart where you can record the novels you've read and the date you finished them. You could drastically cut the cost factor by using your public library.

4. **To spend more time with my family, starting immediately.**

   This is a nice statement of intent (like a New Year's resolution) that has little likelihood of producing meaningful results. It needs to be much more specific and would need agreement and commitment from the rest of the family. (In this case, time would not be a cost since time spent is the result you're looking for.)

Suggested: To spend a minimum of one weekend day per month with family planned activities, beginning immediately, at an average out of pocket cost not to exceed $35.00 per occasion.

5. **To learn five different square dances by September 1st, 20__ .**

Since you've related this to a specific course of instruction, this goal statement would be all right simply by adding the cost factors.

Suggested: To learn five different square dances by September 1st, 20___, spending three hours per week for the next eight weeks, for a total cost of $50.00.

6. **To get a better job.**

This goal is too large and too general.

153

Suggested: Break it down into smaller, more specific components before tackling this goal.

To obtain career counselling and decide which two careers I might pursue By May 1, 20___ .

An additional goal could be:

Suggested: To speak to at least three mid-management people in marketing to find out what they like and dislike about their jobs and how they reached the level of position they're in now. I'll complete this by May 15th, 20___ .

7. **To get more education by the end of the year.**

As there are no quantitative and qualitative measures, nor time deadlines - you're not likely to meet this goal.

Suggested: I'll complete and obtain an above 70 mark in three courses towards a certificate in Computer Programming at the Computer Institute before June 17, 20___ .

Guidelines for setting personal goals

The first kind of goal setting you could try is personal goals. Here are some guidelines that will keep you on track:

1. **Your goals must belong to you and be your individual goal.**

   You're more likely to accomplish personal goals that you set for yourself than if you strive to achieve goals others want you to accomplish. This doesn't mean you can't accept the goals of your spouse, a friend or boss as yours. Consciously think and talk through the advantages and disadvantages of working towards a goal before deciding to pursue it. Prior knowledge of who you are and what you want, is essential, so you can establish goals based on your own internalised values

2. **Goals need to be clear, concrete and written.**

   The purpose of writing goals is to clarify and make them concrete for yourself. Writing and revising goals also forces you

155

to make a commitment to yourself. Once you've written a goal, you'll have more invested in it than before. Writing keeps the goal in front of you and reduces the chance you'll forget about it, as new problems and challenges appear. It helps integrate your goals into projects and identifies conflicting goals. It also takes the emotion out of goal setting and forces you to stand back and be more objective.

3. Start with short range goals.

Learning involves making mistakes as well as achieving success. Start your goal-setting by working on some short range goals that are easily attainable. Short range goals are more likely to be within your control. As you accomplish these, you'll gain more confidence to tackle the more challenging long-range goals. Don't concern yourself if you have to revise your first statement of goals more than once. Life is not stable and situations do change.

4. Consider legality, morality and ethics in your goals.

156

Most peoples' value systems include some degree of concern with the legality, morality and ethics of their actions. You should consider these before you commit yourself to a goal. This would include such situations as cheating on an exam or misleading others in a harmful way.

5. Goals require realism and should be attainable.

Having a goal is the first step to action. However, if your goal is unrealistic or un-attainable - it's not even a goal - but fantasy and daydreaming. The higher the goal; the stronger the motivation. However, if you don't believe accomplishment is possible, there's probably no motivation. If it feels right and makes sense to you and your respected friends, then your goal *is* possible.

6. Specific time deadlines aid in accomplish-ment of goals.

Assigning target dates for completing each step of a plan, provides constant

157

reinforcement and a sense of accomplishment that can help maintain your motivation. You can and should adjust dates, but make sure your excuses are authentic. Put crucial dates such as deadlines into your daytimer.

You might find it helpful to write yourself a contract - stating what you're going to do. Give it to a friend so you won't renege. Then, have a contract-burning ceremony or party when you achieve your goal. This kind of contract is especially helpful when you're trying to stop smoking or want to lose weight.

Guidelines for setting career goals

What is a career? The word 'career' has a negative connotation to many people. It conjures up the image of someone totally dedicated to work, someone who always has his or her nose to the grindstone. If this image has put you off the idea of setting career goals, consider the following definitions - and think again.

A job is a position with specific duties and responsibilities. For example, teaching Grade 3 at Hillside Elementary School is a job.

An occupation is a group of similar jobs in society. It's a broad category that may or may not be specific to a particular company, government department organisation, industry or profession (teacher, engineer, accountant, personal assistant, carpenter, plumber, etc.).

A career includes all your work-related experience, including both paid and unpaid labour. Work-related experience includes full and part-time work, parenting and homemaking, volunteer and community work, hobbies and other leisure activities that may influence a person's work now or in the future. People may change jobs or even occupations, but each person has only one career. A job is what you do with your days - a career is what you do with your life!

Career steps

There are five major steps in planning a career:

159

1. Obtain career counselling and identify your transferrable skills:

If you find that you have trouble motivating yourself or you have little or no incentive to do a good job, you owe it to yourself and your company to change jobs.

Many people stay in an unsatisfactory job because they simply don't know what else they'd like to do. You should find a career counsellor while you're still employed. You'll likely find these through your local government or at universities and colleges.

Qualified career counsellors can help you decide which careers will use, not only your existing skills, but your potential skills as well. They can help you identify your transferrable skills that can you can use in a myriad of occupations. Transferrable skills are those skills you can take from one occupational field into another. For example, supervisory skills, interpersonal skills, accounting knowledge, aptitude with figures and scheduling skills are all transferrable skills. This will allow new horizons to open up for you.

You might consider our career counselling service, found on:

www.dealingwithdifficultpeople.info/uniqu e-career-counselling-service

2. Choose your career:

After rating your strengths, weaknesses, your likes and dislikes and make many choices, you'll likely come up with several choices of occupations. Choose two or three occupations. Your next step is to determine if there is a market for those careers. Talk to at least two or three people in each of your chosen occupations. This is necessary because one may be in the wrong profession. Ask them:

- What do you like about your job?
- What do you dislike about your job?
- What is your normal day like? What tasks do you perform?
- How did you get to the position you're in.

- What education and experience were necessary?
- If you could to do it over, would you still choose that profession?

3. Return to learning:

Then, you'll want to plan where and when you'll receive the necessary training or education, what kind of company will provide the proper on-the-job training (if applicable) what knowledge you'll need before being ready for the next step up.

4. Find a vacant position:

This can be through word-of-mouth or through an advertisement in the newspaper or on-line. Some find a position through employment agencies. (In most countries, employment agencies don't charge the applicant - they charge the employer. So apply at several: it won't cost you anything for their help). If you're applying to an advertisement, circle the verbs or action words they use. Then use those action words in your resume and covering letter. This will give you an edge over other candidates. Answer all questions asked in the advertisement. Recruiters look for similarities between your qualifications and the job requirements (but don't lie!) Every new job applied for, should have a custom-built resume.

5. Apply for the job:

Many people don't use a resume. They fill in an application form and hope it will represent them well. Unfortunately, it doesn't - so use a resume - a good one that 'sells' your unique talents and abilities. This applies to blue- and pink-collar as well as white-collar workers!

6. Attend an interview:

Usually, the only thing representing you before an interview is your resume. If it isn't 'up to par,' you likely won't be asked to come for an interview. If they ask you to come for an interview, remember that you're there to 'sell' yourself - don't let shyness keep you from 'tooting your horn.' Know your strengths and weaknesses and be ready to discuss them with the

163

interviewer. Have your facts clear in your mind, expect their questions and have information handy that they may need.

Know as much as you can about their company - its products and service. Make sure your physical appearance is neat and clean and that your apparel suits the position for which you're applying. Never, under any circumstances, wear old jeans or cords to an interview. Blue-collar workers may wear clean jeans and cords, but if you're an office worker wear apparel one step up from the vacant position. The interviewer knows that you'll be better dressed than you would be on the job. So if you come in wearing an outfit with stains on it or needs pressing, they know you'll be wearing something even worse when you're on the job.

Remember that you only have one chance to make a good first impression. Most employers decide whether they're going to hire you within the first four minutes of the interview. Your physical appearance plays a large role in that decision-making.

7. Send a thank-you note:

Follow-up with a thank you note to the interviewer. This will set you apart from other applicants.

8. Start your new job.

How can I start to plan my goals?

Life inventory

To find out where you want to go, you have to know where you are now and what your desires are. To help with this, complete the following on a piece of paper. List everything that comes to mind; don't censor anything. Consider asking a friend to help after you make an initial list.

1. Peak experiences I've had:

List the special moments in your life. They don't have to be the most exquisite moments you've ever had. There are or have been particular times when you felt you were really living and enjoying life to the fullest (self-actualisation).

2. Peak experiences I'd like to have:

165

These are situations you want to happen to you (a kind of 'bucket list'). Also list here peak experiences you'd like to have again.

3. Things I do well:

Quickly list your strengths. Notice that things you do well aren't always that fulfilling.

4. Things I do poorly:

Note these activities that you do not do well, but for some reason you want to or have to do them. However, don't list activities that you have no interest in doing or don't need to do.

5. Things I'd like to stop doing:

Do you have habits you consider bad? Are there things you have to do, but don't want to do?

6. Things I'd like to learn to do well:

What do you want to learn? What must you learn if you are to meet your goals?

7. Things I'd like to start doing now!

Be creative - dream a little!

Planning:

To start your planning, write down the following (be specific):

1. What are your lifetime goals? Make separate lists for personal, family, social, financial, spiritual and community goals. Give each portion of your goals time limits.
2. Then prioritise each list, 1, 2, 3, etc.
3. To help yourself define these goals, consider,
   a. If you could live anywhere in the world, where would that be?
   b. If you could have any kind of job or career you wanted, what would you want to do?
   c. What goals do you expect to reach within 2 years?
   d. How would you spend your life if you knew you had only 6 months left to live? (You have an inoperable aneurism, but will be healthy until the last).
   e. If you found out you had 24 hours to live, what would be the 5 most important things you'd want to do?

167

On question 3 (d), did you put down that you'd likely travel or spend more time with your family? That's what most people jot down here. Whatever you've identified in this question identifies what is truly important to you. If you said you'd spend more time with your family - why aren't you doing that now, instead of waiting until it's forced upon you? If you want to travel - why aren't you making plans now to make it happen?

Goal setting plan

When setting any life or career goals for myself, I use the following plan to keep myself on track and make my goals far more concrete. It's very simplistic, but it works. Steps 4, 5 and 6 will keep you heading in the right direction and help you reach your goal.

Step 1: Describe the situation as it is now (what you're doing now).

Step 2: Describe the ideal situation (what you'd like to be doing).

Step 3: Identify the gap between 1 and 2. (This is your goal, which should fill the gap.)

168

Step 4:List the driving and restraining forces. (Driving forces describe the benefits you'll derive when you reach your goal. Restraining forces are the obstacles that may be in your way that may keep you from reaching your goal. What problems might you face? What are the possible spin-off problems?)

Step 5: List ways you will overcome the restraining forces. (This is where you'll brainstorm.)

Step 6: Formulate a plan of action that includes these four headings:

Step:
Date or Time Limit:
People to Involve:
Resources Required.

Step 7: Implement your plan of action

Step 8: Evaluate the success of implementing your plan.

Driving & restraining forces

In Step 4, it's important to identify the driving and restraining forces. These lists give a clear picture of the benefits you'll have when your goal is achieved. For instance if your goal was to lose weight, you'd read your driving force list when you're tempted to take that piece of chocolate cake. By identifying the restraining forces, you'll be fully aware of the problems you might face. This enables you to come up with a plan of action that will help you go over, under, around or through obstacles that get in your way.

Here's an example of how you could identify driving and restraining forces. Let's say you've set your goal to lose ten pounds and want to do so by August 1st, 20___. Identify the driving forces that will keep you striving to obtain your goal and the restraining forces, so you will know what you're up against.

The following will give you an example of how you would do this if you were trying to lose weight:

Driving Forces:

I'll be healthier.
I can buy new clothes.

170

I'll feel better.
I'll live longer.
I'll be in better shape physically
I can do more.

Restraining Forces:

I like to eat!
My friends eat a lot too!
I'll have to buy new clothes.
Food and exercise plan may cost more.
I'll have to exercise!
I'll have to starve!

Rules for brainstorming

Step 5 is important because it enables you to find ways of overcoming your restraining forces. To do this, try brainstorming to come up with unique or creative ways to eliminate your restraining forces.

Brainstorming started in the workplace and normally involves groups of people. It's a way of coming up with very unique ways of solving problems. The advantage of using brainstorming is that not only do you come up with Plan A, but Plan B and C as well. Many

171

job-finding groups find brainstorming an invaluable tool. Whether you're brainstorming alone or in a group, for business or home life, use these guidelines:

1. Concentrate on one restraining force at a time.

2. Encourage idea quantity. At this point, quality is not considered important. What you're seeking is as many ideas and suggestions as possible.

3. In group brainstorming, discourage critical judgment and evaluation. No one is allowed to say, *'That won't work because ...'* during a brainstorming session (not even you!) You're looking for ways of getting ideas, not trying to suppress them. Someone's idea (which really won't work) just might be the idea that triggers someone else to think of one that will work.

4. Encourage *wild thinking* and build on an idea. Offer any idea, no matter how questionable and encourage the group (or yourself) to build on ideas, altering, expanding and changing them. The purpose

172

here is to get ideas, not to pass judgment on them.

5. During the actual brainstorming (which is of very short duration) there should be no side discussions. All members of the group are to concentrate their energies on coming up with additional ideas.

6. In group discussions, don't allow outside observers. Everyone in the room has to participate. Everyone should offer at least two suggestions during the session.

7. The brainstorming session itself should not last less than five minutes or more than fifteen. Shorter lengths of time don't allow enough good ideas to surface and after fifteen minutes, the greater portion of the ideas become clearly impractical.

8. One member of the group should take notes, recording the ideas as fast as they're offered. When working in groups it's a good idea to have the suggestions listed on a flip chart where everyone can see them. Previous ideas lead to further suggestions.

9. Have an idea or two in the back of your head to get the session started. This will

provide a trigger to get the session moving. Once it begins, the ideas come fast and furiously.

In our example of losing weight, one of the restraining forces was that your friends and co-workers eat a lot too. Let's say you normally have coffee with your friends every morning and you've been in the habit of buying gooey cinnamon buns. If you want to lose weight, it's not going to be easy for you to resist if you have coffee break with them. You might have to grab an apple and walk around the block for coffee break to get through it. This way, you've removed one of the restraining forces that might have kept you from reaching your goal. In addition you'll have had some exercise and a healthy snack. You'll need to tackle each restraining force so you can remove all possible obstacles.

Using the goal setting plan

To describe how the process works, here is an example of a goal taken through the process:

Step 1: The situation as it is now

I have no supervisory experience or training.

Step 2: The ideal situation

I need supervisory training so I'll be prepared for a future supervisory promotion.

Step 3: The gap (or goal)

To obtain supervisory training. (A general goal). I'll complete and obtain an above 70 mark in one course towards a Business Administration Certificate by March 15, 20__. (A specific goal).

Step 4: List the Driving and Restraining forces

Driving forces: (Benefits of reaching the goal)

- I'll be ready for a promotion.
- I want to learn, am ready to learn.
- I'll earn more money.
- I'll gain more status.
- I'll use my abilities better.
- I feel I can do it.
- My employer, co-workers and family have offered their help.

175

Restraining forces: (Obstacles to overcome)

a) I'm not sure what courses to take.
b) It will cost money.
c) I'll have less time for my family.
d) I've forgotten how to study and will have too many family distractions.
e) I could have problems with transportation and parking.
f) It's a long term goal; can I do it?
g) I won't have time to do everything I have to do.

Step 5: Determine ways to overcome restraining forces

The results of brainstorming in this example are:

a) I'll talk to the representatives at Smith College and Jasper University to determine what courses I should take and how much each of those choices will cost.
b) I'll talk to my employer to see if my company will help me with the cost of training.
c) I'll determine how I can eliminate all the extra activities that take me away from my

family and from obtaining the training I need.

d) It will take time to re-learn the skill of studying - so I'll ask for my family's co-operation to give me uninterrupted study time.

e) I'll arrange to have the car and organise parking for the nights I'm attending classes.

f) I'll keep myself motivated by taking only one course at a time instead of worrying about all ten of them at once.

g) I'll resign from the condominium board so I'll have more time to spend with my family and to take courses.

Step 6: Formulate a plan of action that includes these four headings:

Step: Contact college re: courses and parking
Date or Time Limit: tomorrow
People to Involve: college rep.
Resources Required: phone / rep

Step: Contact university
Date or Time Limit: tomorrow
People to Involve: university rep
Resources Required: phone / rep

Step: Decide which course I'll take and costs
Date or Time Limit: within 2 days
People to Involve: boss
Resources Required: boss's time

Step: Talk to family – ask for help around the house
Date or Time Limit: within 3 days
People to Involve: family
Resources Required: family's time

Step: Talk to spouse re: use of car
Date or Time Limit: within 3 days
People to Involve: spouse
Resources Required: his/her time

Step: Sign up for selected courses
Date or Time Limit: within 4 days
People to Involve: college / university rep.
Resources Required: rep's time

Step: Talk to family re: help in obtaining uninterrupted study time
Date or Time Limit: within 3 days
People to Involve: family
Resources Required: family's time

Step 7: Implement your plan of action

Step 8: Evaluate the success of implementing your plan.

Goal setting won't get you that job or allow you to take that trip you've dreamed about. But putting your plan into action will. Don't allow yourself to get lazy. Keep your momentum going by realising that you're constantly moving closer to your 'dream job or dream vacation.' Learn to be flexible, bounce with the punches and keep your eyes open for unexpected opportunities that might surface.

Now it's time to put words into action. Write down several short-term goals you'd like to reach. Before using the Goal Setting Guide, ask yourself the following questions:

a) Is my goal specific? Can I tell when I've reached my goal?

b) Is it a tangible (something you can see) or intangible (relating to behaviour and feelings) goal?

c) Is it truly a short-term goal or will it take a long time to accomplish this goal?

179

The hardest goals to reach are those that are too general to gauge when you've achieved them or intangible goals. People often run out of steam when accomplishing long-term goals, so they must persevere by cutting their goal down to short-term ones. Then:

1. Go through the 8 steps of the goal setting process.
2. Follow the guidelines and reach your goals.
3. Don't forget to have a back-up goal ready to take over when you're close to reaching your first goal.

Goal setting - intensive goal setting - is hard work. It takes a lot of effort and time, but it's worth it. If it takes you two years to decide where you want to go, that's okay, as long as you're steadily working towards finding the right occupation and lifestyle for you. Good luck with your goal setting.

CONCLUSION

You now have the tools that will enable you to deal with time problems. These essential skills will help you to handle all types of time pressures. Learn these skills and you can't help but improve your ability to pack more activities into your busy day. It will allow you to have some time for yourself to do what you've decided is important to you.

Now it's time to sit down and do some critical planning. Analyse ways you can use your time better and establish concrete, written, realistic goals for yourself.

You will now know how to:

- Accomplish what you want in life,
- Live a longer, fuller life,
- Set priorities (yours) and follow them,
- Stop procrastinating,
- Overcome the fear of failure or success,
- Say 'no' when someone tries to force you to do something you don't want to do,
- To prevent interruptions and crisis,

- To use proven business practices at home as well as at work,
- Set concrete, written, realistic goals for yourself - both career and personal,

Learn the techniques and practise them daily. They do work! Like any new skill, however, you need to use them consistently until they're automatic. When you've mastered them, you can look forward to being able to control how you deal with time in your busy world.

If you use these skills, you'll need to be prepared for success, because success will inevitably follow!

UNIQUE CAREER COUNSELLING SERVICE

Available via e-mail

Provided by Roberta Cava of:

Cava Consulting,
105 / 3 Township Drive,
Burleigh Heads, Queensland.
4220, Australia.

In these hard economic times, are you finding it difficult to find suitable employment in your field of work? How would you like to expand those opportunities? This unique career counselling service will enable you to determine your transferrable skills and identify another 20 to 40 occupations where you could use those skills.

An investment of **$175.00** (Aus) will provide you with an extensive report that includes:

- A list of your transferrable skills
- 20 to 30 primary and secondary occupations you could investigate that use your transferrable skills

183

- A psychological report that includes:

1. Your strengths in the areas of interest, ability, values, personality, capacity
2. Interest, ability and personality profiles
3. What you think your skills are compared to what they really are
4. Determine your management, persuasive, social artistic, clerical, mechanical, investigative and operational abilities
5. Whether you are outgoing, reserved, factual, creative, analytical, caring organised or causal
6. Your ability to think, reason and solve problems
7. Values inventory
8. Your stamina level
9. Your I.Q. Score
10. Performance and personality characteristics
11. Motivational and De-motivational factors
12. Whether you have what it takes to become an entrepreneur and have your own business

What will Happen?

After payment is made, you will be able to download a PowerPoint set of questions that you will complete. Some of the questions are timed and every question must be answered.

Your transferrable skills	10 questions
What do you like to do?	7
Timed Test (22 minutes):	30
Likes and Dislikes:	35
What kind of job do you prefer?	40
What kind of person are you?	11
How do you compare with others?	31
Describe your personality	23
Which do you prefer	15
Your preferences	8
Personality Profile	<u>40</u>
Total	**255**

When you have completed the questions, you will e-mail the file to Roberta Cava. She will then do an analysis of your answers and e-mail you a detailed report (approximately 15 pages) including:

- Your interests and abilities
- Personality career reference results
- Capacity Score

- IQ Score
- Entrepreneurial profile results
- Values Inventory
- Job/Career Listings
- Samples of jobs based on applicant's tendencies
  - Primary
  - Secondary
- Personality Profile
  - Personality in workplace
  - Personality at home
- General characteristics
  - Secondary characteristics
- Leadership method
- Decision-making method
- Stamina
- Performance Characteristics
- Personality Characteristics
- Motivational factors
- De-motivational factors

If you're interested in participating in this unique career counselling service, please go to our web page and follow the prompts:

186

www.dealingwithdifficultpeople.info/unique-career-counselling-service

For more information, contact Roberta Cava at:

rcava@dealingwithdifficultpeople.info

BIBLIOGRAPHY

Covey, Stephen R., *The 7 Habits of highly successful people,* Simon & Schuster.

Lakein, Alan, *How to get control of your time and your life,* New American Library, 1996.

McKenzie, R. Alex, *The Time Trap, The Classic Book on Time Management,* AMACOM, 2009.

McRae, Bradley C., *Practical Time Management; How to get more things done in less time,* Self Counsel Press, 1993.

Zeller, Dirk, *Successful Time Management for Dummies,* John Wiley & Sons, 2008.